TABLE OF CONTENTS

PREFACE.

The following pages are a translation of that portion of Professor Ferri's volume on Criminal Sociology which is immediately concerned with the practical problems of criminality. The Report of the Government committee appointed to inquire into the treatment of habitual drunkards, the Report of the committee of inquiry into the best means of identifying habitual criminals, the revision of the English criminal returns, the Reports of committees appointed to inquire into the administration of prisons and the best methods of dealing with habitual offenders, vagrants, beggars, inebriate and juvenile delinquents, are all evidence of the fact that the formidable problem of crime is again pressing its way to the front and demanding re-examination at the hands of the present generation. The real dimensions of the question, as Professor Ferri points out, are partially hidden by the superficial interpretations which are so often placed upon the returns relating to crime. If the population of prisons or penitentiaries should happen to be declining, this is immediately interpreted to mean that crime is on the decrease. And yet a cursory examination of the facts is sufficient to show that a decrease in the prison population is merely the result of shorter sentences and the substitution of fines or other similar penalties for imprisonment. If the list of offences for trial before a judge and jury should exhibit any symptoms of diminution, this circumstance is immediately seized upon as a proof that the criminal population is declining, and yet the diminution may merely arise from the fact that large numbers of cases which used to be tried before a jury are now dealt with summarily by a magistrate. In other words, what we witness is a change of judicial procedure, but not necessarily a decrease of crime. Again, when it is pointed out that the number of persons for trial for indictable offences in England and Wales amounted to 53,044 in 1874-8 and 56,472 in 1889-93, we are at a loss to see what colour these figures give to the statement that there has been a real and substantial decrease of crime. The increase, it is true, may not be keeping pace with the growth of the general population, but, as an eminent judge recently stated from the bench, this is to be accounted for by the fact that the public is every year becoming more lenient and more unwilling to prosecute. But an increase of leniency, however excellent in itself, is not to be confounded with a decrease of crime. In the study of social phenomena our paramount duty is to look at facts and not appearances.

But whether criminality is keeping pace with the growth of population or not it is a problem of great magnitude all the same, and it will not be solved, as Professor Ferri points out, by a mere resort to punishments of greater rigour and severity. On this matter he is at one with the Scotch departmental committee appointed to inquire into the best means of dealing with habitual offenders, vagrants, and juveniles. As far as the suppression of vagrancy is concerned the members of the committee are unanimously of opinion that ``the severest enactments of the general law are futile, and that the best results have been obtained by the milder provisions of more recent statutes." They also speak of the ``utter inadequacy of the present system in all the variety of detail which it offers to deter the habitual offender from a course of life which devolves the cost of his maintenance on the prison and the poorhouse when he is not preying directly on the public." The committee state that they have had testimony from a large number of witnesses supporting the view that ``long sentences of imprisonment effect no good result," and they arrive at the conclusion that to double the present sentences would not diminish the number of habitual offenders. In this conclusion they are at one with the views of the Royal Commission on Penal Servitude, which acquiesced in the objection to the penal servitude system on the ground that it ``not only fails to reform offenders, but in the case of the less hardened criminals and especially first offenders produces a deteriorating effect." A similar opinion was recently expressed by the Prisons Committee presided over by Mr. Herbert Gladstone. As soon as punishment reaches a point at which it makes men worse than they were before, it becomes useless as an instrument of reformation or social defence.

The proper method of arriving at a more or less satisfactory solution of the criminal problem is to inquire into the causes which are producing the criminal population, and to institute remedies based upon the results of such an inquiry. Professor Ferri's volume has this object in view. The first chanter, on the data of Criminal Anthropology, is an inquiry into the individual conditions which tend to produce criminal habits of mind and action. The second chapter, on the data of criminal statistics, is an examination of the adverse social conditions which tend to drive certain sections of the population into crime. It is Professor Ferri's contention that the volume of crime will not be materially diminished by codes of criminal law however skilfully they may be constructed, but by an amelioration of the adverse individual and social conditions of the community as a whole. Crime is a product of these adverse conditions, and the only effective way of grappling with it is to do away as far as possible with the causes from which it springs. Although criminal codes can do comparatively little towards the reduction of crime, they are absolutely essential for the protection of society. Accordingly, the last chapter, on Practical Reforms, is intended to show how criminal law and prison administration may be made more effective for purposes of social defence.

W. D. M.

INTRODUCTION.

THE POSITIVE SCHOOL OF CRIMINAL LAW.

During the past twelve or fourteen years Italy has poured forth a stream of new ideas on the subject of crime and criminals; and only the short-sightedness of her enemies or the vanity of her flatterers can fail to recognise in this stream something more than the outcome of individual labours.

A new departure in science is a simple phenomenon of nature, determined in its origin and progress, like all such phenomena, by conditions of time and place. Attention must be drawn to these conditions at the outset, for it is only by accurately defining them that the scientific conscience of the student of sociology is developed and confirmed.

The experimental philosophy of the latter half of our century, combined with human biology and psychology, and with the natural study of human society, had already produced an intellectual atmosphere decidedly favourable to a practical inquiry into the criminal manifestations of individual and social life.

To these general conditions must be added the plain and everyday contrast between the metaphysical perfection of criminal law and the progressive increase of crime, as well as the contrast between legal theories of crime and the study of the mental characteristics of a large number of criminals.

From this point onwards, nothing could be more natural than the rise of a new school, whose object was to make an experimental study of social pathology in respect of its criminal symptoms, in order to bring theories of crime and punishment into harmony with everyday facts. This is the positive school of criminal law, whereof the fundamental purpose is to study the natural genesis of criminality in the criminal, and in the physical and social conditions of his life, so as to apply the most effectual remedies to the various causes of crime.

Thus we are not concerned merely with the construction of a theory of anthropology or psychology, or a system of criminal statistics, nor merely with the setting of abstract legal theories against other theories which are still more abstract. Our task is to show that the basis of every theory concerning the self-defence of the community against evil-doers must be the observation of the individual and of society in their criminal activity. In one word, our task is to construct a criminal sociology.

For, as it seems to me, all that general sociology can do is to furnish the more ordinary and universal inferences concerning the life of communities; and upon this canvas the several sciences of sociology are delineated by the specialised observation of each distinct order of social facts. In this manner we may construct a political sociology, an economic sociology, a legal sociology, by studying the special laws of normal or social activity amongst human beings, after previously studying the more general laws of individual and collective existence. And thus we may construct a criminal sociology, by studying, with such an aim and by such a method, the abnormal and anti-social actions of human beings--or, in other words, by studying crime and criminals.

Neither the Romans, great exponents as they were of the civil law, nor the practical spirits of the Middle Ages, had been able to lay down a philosophic system of criminal law. It was Beccaria, influenced far more by sentiment than by scientific precision, who gave a great impetus to the doctrine of crimes and punishments by summarising the ideas and sentiments of his age.[1] Out of the various germs contained in his generous initiative there has been developed, to his well-deserved credit, the classical school of criminal law.

[1] Desjardins, in the Introduction to his ``Cahiers des Etats Generaux en 1789 et la Legislation Criminelle," Paris, 1883, gives a good description of the state of public opinion in that age. He speaks also of the charges which were brought against the advocates of the new doctrines concerning crime, that they upset the moral and social order of things. Nowadays, charges against the experimental school are cited from these same advocates; for the revolutionary of yesterday is very often the conservative of to-day.

This school had, and still has, a practical purpose, namely, to diminish all punishments, and to abolish a certain number, by a magnanimous reaction of humanity against the arbitrary harshness of mediaeval times. It had also, and still has, a method of its own, namely, to study crime from its first principles, as an abstract entity dependent upon law.

Here and there since the time of Beccaria another stream of theory has made itself manifest. Thus there is the correctional school, which Roeder brought into special prominence not many years ago. But though it flourished in Germany, less in Italy and France, and somewhat more in Spain, it had no long existence as an independent school, for it was only too easily confuted by the close sequence of inexorable facts. Moreover, it could do no more than oppose a few humanitarian arguments on the reformation of offenders to the traditional arguments of the theories of jurisprudence, of absolute and relative justice, of intimidation, utility, and the like.

No doubt the principle that punishment ought to have a reforming effect upon the criminal survives as a rudimentary organ in nearly all the schools which concern themselves with crime. But this is only a secondary principle, and as it were the indirect object of punishment; and besides, the observations of anthropology, psychology, and criminal statistics have finally disposed of it, having established the fact that, under any system of punishment, with the most severe or the most indulgent methods, there are always certain types of criminals, representing a large number of individuals, in regard to whom amendment is simply impossible, or very transitory, on account of their organic and moral degeneration. Nor must we forget that, since the natural roots of crime spring not only from the individual organism, but also, in large measure, from its physical and social environment, correction of the individual is not sufficient to prevent relapse if we do not also, to the best of our ability, reform the social environment. The utility and the duty of reformation none the less survive, even for the positive school, whenever it is possible, and for certain classes of criminals; but, as a fundamental principle of a scientific theory, it has passed away.

Hitherto, then, the classical school stands alone, with varying shades of opinion, but one and distinct as a method, and as a body of principles and consequences. And whilst it has achieved its aim in the most recent penal codes, with a great, and too frequently an excessive diminution of punishments, so in respect of theory, in Italy, Germany, and France it has crowned its work with a series of masterpieces amongst which I will only mention Carrara's ``Programme of Criminal Law." As the author tells us in one of his later editions, from the a priori principle that ``crime is a fact dependent upon law, an infraction rather than an action," he deduced--and that by the sheer force of an admirable logic--a complete symmetrical scheme of legal and abstract consequences, wherein judges are compelled, whether they like it or not, to determine the position of every criminal who comes before them.

But now the classical school, which sprang from the marvellous little work of Beccaria, has completed its historic cycle. It has yielded all it could, and writers of the present day who still cling to it can only recast the old material. The youngest of them, indeed, are condemned to a sort of Byzantine discussion of scholastic formulas, and to a sterile process of scientific rumination.

And meantime, outside our universities and academies, criminality continues to grow, and the punishments hitherto inflicted, though they can neither protect nor indemnify the honest, succeed in corrupting and degrading evil-doers. And whilst our treatises and codes (which are too often mere treatises cut up into segments) lose themselves in the fog of their legal abstractions, we feel more strongly every day, in police courts and at assizes, the necessity for those biological and sociological studies of crime and criminals which, when logically directed, can throw light as nothing else can upon the administration of the penal law.

CHAPTER I.

THE DATA OF CRIMINAL ANTHROPOLOGY.

The experimental school of criminal sociology took its original title from its studies of anthropology; it is still commonly regarded as little more than a ``criminal anthropology school." And though this title no longer corresponds with the development of the school, which also takes into account and investigates the data of psychology, statistics, and sociology, it is none the less true that the most characteristic impetus of the new scientific movement was due to anthropological studies. This was conspicuously the case when Lombroso, giving a scientific form to sundry scattered and fragmentary observations upon criminals, added fresh life to them by a collection of inquiries which were not only original but also governed by a distinct idea, and established the new science of criminal anthropology.

It is possible, of course, to discover a very early origin for criminal anthropology, as for general anthropology; for, as Pascal said, man has always been the most wonderful object of study to himself. For observations on physiognomy in particular we may go as far backwards as to Plato, and his comparisons of the human face and character with those of the brutes, or even to Aristotle, who still earlier observed the physical and psychological correspondence between the passions of men and their facial expression. And after the mediaeval gropings in chiromancy, metoscopy, podomancy and so forth, one comes to the seventeenth century studies in physiognomy by the Jesuit Niquetius, by Cortes, Cardanus, De la Chambre, Della Porta, &c., who were precursors of Gall, Spurzheim, and Lavater on one side, and, on the other, of the modern scientific study of the emotions, with their expression in face and gesture, conducted by Camper, Bell, Engel, Burgess, Duchenne, Gratiolet, Piderit, Mantegazza, Schaffhausen, Schack, Heiment, and above all by Darwin.

With regard to the special observation of criminals, over and above the limited statements of the old physiognomists and phrenologists, Lauvergne (1841) in France and Attomyr (1842) in Germany had accurately applied the theories of Gall to the examination of convicts; and their works, in spite of certain exaggerations of phrenology, are still a valuable treasury of observations in anthropology. In Italy, De Rolandis (1835) had published his observations on a deceased criminal; in America, Sampson (1846) had traced the connection between criminality and cerebral organisation; in Germany, Camper (1854) published a study on the physiognomy of murderers; and Ave Lallemant (1858-62) produced a long work on criminals, from the psychological point of view.

But the science of criminal anthropology, more strictly speaking, only begins with the observations of English gaol surgeons and other learned men, such as Forbes Winslow (1854), Mayhew (1860), Thomson (1870), Wilson (1870), Nicolson

(1872), Maudsley (1873), and with the very notable work of Despine (1868), which indeed gave rise to the inquiries of Thomson, and which, in spite of its lack of synthetic treatment and systematic unity, is still, taken in conjunction with the work of Ave Lallemant, the most important inquiry in the psychological domain anterior to the work of Lombroso.

Nevertheless, it was only with the first edition of ``The Criminal'' (1876) that criminal anthropology asserted itself as an independent science, distinct from the main trunk of general anthropology, itself quite recent in its origin, having come into existence with the works of Daubenton, Blumenbach, Soemmering, Camper, White, and Pritchard.

The work of Lombroso set out with two original faults: the mistake of having given undue importance, at any rate apparently, to the data of craniology and anthropometry, rather than to those of psychology; and, secondly, that of having mixed up, in the first two editions, all criminals in a single class. In later editions these defects were eliminated, Lombroso having adopted the observation which I made in the first instance, as to the various anthropological categories of criminals. This does not prevent certain critics of criminal anthropology from repeating, with a strange monotony, the venerable objections as to the ``impossibility of distinguishing a criminal from an honest man by the shape of his skull,'' or of ``measuring human responsibility in accordance with different craniological types.''[2]

[2] Vol. ii. of the fourth edition of ``The Criminal'' (1889) is specially concerned with the epileptic and idiotic criminal (referred to alcoholism, hysteria, mattoidism) whether occasional or subject to violent impulse; whilst vol. i. is concerned only with congenital criminality and moral insanity.

But these original faults in no way obscure the two following noteworthy facts-- that within a few years after the publication of ``The Criminal'' there were published, in Italy and elsewhere, a whole library of studies in criminal anthropology, and that a new school has been established, having a distinct method and scientific developments, which are no longer to be looked for in the classical school of criminal law.

I.

What, then, is criminal anthropology? And of what nature are its fundamental data, which lead us up to the general conclusions of criminal sociology?

If general anthropology is, according to the definition of M. de Quatrefages, the natural history of man, as zoology is the natural history of animals, criminal anthropology is but the study of a single variety of mankind. In other words, it is the natural history of the criminal man.

Criminal anthropology studies the criminal man in his organic and psychical constitution, and in his life as related to his physical and social environment--just as anthropology has done for man in general, and for the various races of mankind. So that, as already said, whilst the classical observers of crime study various offences in their abstract character, on the assumption that the criminal, apart from particular cases which are evident and appreciable, is a man of the ordinary type, under normal conditions of intelligence and feeling, the anthropological observers of crime, on the other hand, study the criminal first of all by means of direct observations, in anatomical and physiological laboratories, in prisons and madhouses, organically and physically, comparing him with the typical characteristics of the normal man, as well as with those of the mad and the degenerate.

Before recounting the general data of criminal anthropology, it is necessary to lay particular stress upon a remark which I made in the original edition of this work, but which our opponents have too frequently ignored.

We must carefully discriminate between the technical value of anthropological data concerning the criminal man and their scientific function in criminal sociology.

For the student of criminal anthropology, who builds up the natural history of the criminal, every characteristic has an anatomical, or a physiological, or a psychological value in itself, apart from the sociological conclusions which it may be possible to draw from it. The technical inquiry into these bio- psychical characteristics is the special work of this new science of criminal anthropology.

Now these data, which are the conclusions of the anthropologist, are but starting-points for the criminal sociologist, from which he has to reach his legal and social conclusions. Criminal anthropology is to criminal sociology, in its scientific function, what the biological sciences, in description and experimentation, are to clinical practice.

In other words, the criminal sociologist is not in duty bound to conduct for himself the inquiries of criminal anthropology, just as the clinical operator is not bound to be a physiologist or an anatomist. No doubt the direct observation of criminals is a very serviceable study, even for the criminal sociologist; but the only duty of the latter is to base his legal and social inferences upon the positive data of criminal anthropology for the biological aspects of crime, and upon statistical data for the influences of physical and social environment, instead of contenting himself with mere abstract legal syllogisms.

On the other hand it is clear that sundry questions which have a direct bearing upon criminal anthropology--as, for instance, in regard to some particular biological characteristic, or to its evolutionary significance--have no immediate obligation or value for criminal sociology, which employs only the fundamental and most indubitable data of criminal anthropology. So that it is but a clumsy way of propounding the question to ask, as it is too frequently asked: ``What connection can there be between the cephalic index, or the transverse measurement of a murderer's jaw, and his responsibility for the crime which he has committed?'' The scientific function of the anthropological data is a very different thing, and the only legitimate question which sociology can put to anthropology is this:--``Is the criminal, and in what respects is he, a normal or an abnormal man? And if he is, or when he is abnormal, whence is the abnormality derived? Is it congenital or contracted, capable or incapable of rectification?''

This is all; and yet it is sufficient to enable the student of crime to arrive at positive conclusions concerning the measures which society can take in order to defend itself against crime; whilst he can draw other conclusions from criminal statistics.

As for the principal data hitherto established by criminal anthropology, whilst we must refer the reader for detailed information to the works of specialists, we may repeat that this new science studies the criminal in his organic and in his psychical constitution, for these are the two inseparable aspects of human existence.

A beginning has naturally been made with the organic study of the criminal, both anatomical and physiological, since we must study the organ before the function, and the physical before the moral. This, however, has given rise to a host of misconceptions and one- sided criticisms, which have not yet ceased; for criminal anthropology has been charged, by such as consider only the most conspicuous data with narrowing crime down to the mere result of conformations of the skull or convolutions of the brain. The fact is that purely morphological observations are but preliminary steps to the histological and physiological study of the brain, and of the body as a whole.

As for craniology, especially in regard to the two distinct and characteristic types of criminals--murderers and thieves, an incontestable inferiority has been noted in the shape of the head, by comparison with normal men, together with a greater frequency of hereditary and pathological departures from the normal type. Similarly an examination of the brains of criminals, whilst it reveals in them an inferiority of form and histological type, gives also, in a great majority of cases, indications of disease which were frequently undetected in their lifetime. Thus M. Dally, who for twenty years past has displayed exceptional acumen in problems of this kind, said that ``all the criminals who had been subjected to autopsy (after execution) gave evidence of cerebral injury.''[3]

[3] In a discussion at the Medico-Psychological Society of Paris; ``Proceedings'' for 1881, i. 93, 266, 280, 483.

4

Observations of the physiognomy of criminals, which no one will undervalue who has studied criminals in their lifetime, with adequate knowledge, as well as other physical inquiries, external and internal, have shown the existence of remarkable types, from the greater frequency of the tattooed man to exceptionally abnormal conditions of the frame and the organs, dating from birth, together with many forms of contracted disease.

Finally, inquiries of a physiological nature into the reflex action of the body, and especially into general and specific sensibility, and sensibility to pain, and into reflex action under external agencies, conducted with the aid of instruments which record the results, have shown abnormal conditions, all tending to physical insensibility, deep-seated and more or less absolute, but incontestably different in kind from that which obtains amongst the average men of the same social classes.

These are organic conditions, it must be at once affirmed, which account as nothing else can for the undeniable fact of the hereditary transmission of tendencies to crime, as well as of predisposition to insanity, to suicide, and to other forms of degeneration.

The second division of criminal anthropology, which is by far the more important, with a more direct influence upon criminal sociology, is the psychological study of the criminal. This recognition of its greater importance does not prevent our critics from concentrating their attack upon the organic characterisation of criminals, in oblivion of the psychological characterisation, which even in Lombroso's book occupies the larger part of the text.[4]

[4] A recent example of this infatuation amongst one-sided, and therefore ineffectual critics is the work of Colajanni, ``Socialism and Criminal Sociology," Catania, 1889. In the first volume, which is devoted to criminal anthropology, out of four hundred pages of argumentative criticism (which does not prevent the author from taking our most fundamental conclusions on the anthropological classification of criminals, and on crime, as phenomena of psychical atavism), there are only six pages, 227- 232, for the criticism of psychological types.

Criminal psychology presents us with the characteristics which may be called specially descriptive, such as the slang, the handwriting, the secret symbols, the literature and art of the criminal; and on the other hand it makes known to us the characteristics which, in combination with organic abnormality, account for the development of crime in the individual. And these characteristics are grouped in two psychical and fundamental abnormalities, namely, moral insensibility and want of foresight.

Moral insensibility, which is decidedly more congenital than contracted, is either total or partial, and is displayed in criminals who inflict personal injuries, as much as

5

in others, with a variety of symptoms which I have recorded elsewhere, and which are eventually reduced to these conditions of the moral sense in a large number of criminals--a lack of repugnance to the idea and execution of the offence, previous to its commission, and the absence of remorse after committing it.

Outside of these conditions of the moral sense, which is no special sentiment, but an expression of the entire moral constitution of the individual, as the temperament is of his physiological constitution, other sentiments, of selfishness or even of unselfishness, are not wanting in the majority of criminals. Hence arise many illusions for superficial observers of criminal life. But these latter sentiments are either excessive, as hate, cupidity, vanity and the like, and are thus stimulants to crime, or else, as with religion, love, honour, loyalty, and so on, they cease to be forces antagonistic to crime, because they have no foundation in a normal moral sense.

From this fundamental inferiority of sentiment there follows an inferiority of intelligence, which, however, does not exclude certain forms of craftiness, though it tends to inability to foresee the consequences of crime, far in excess of what is observed in the average members of the classes of society to which the several criminals belong.

Thus the psychology of the criminal is summed up in a defective resistance to criminal tendencies and temptations, due to that ill-balanced impulsiveness which characterises children and savages.

II.

I have long been convinced, by my study of works on criminal anthropology, but especially by direct and continuous observation from a physiological or a psychological point of view of a large number of criminals, whether mad or of normal intelligence, that the data of criminal anthropology are not entirely applicable, in their complete and essential form, to all who commit crimes. They are to be confined to a certain number, who may be called congenital, incorrigible, and habitual criminals. But apart from these there is a class of occasional criminals, who do not exhibit, or who exhibit in slighter degrees, the anatomical, physiological, and psychological characteristics which constitute the type described by Lombroso as ``the criminal man.''

Before further defining these two main classes of criminals, in their natural and descriptive characterisation, I must add a positive demonstration, which can be attested under two distinct forms--(1) by the results of anthropological observation of criminals, and (2) by statistics of relapse, and of the manifestations of crime which anthropologists have hitherto chiefly studied.

6

As for organic anomalies, as I cannot here treat the whole matter in detail, I will simply reproduce from my study of homicide a summary of results for a single category of these anomalies, which a methodical observation of every class of criminals will carry further and render more precise, as Lombroso has already shown (see the fourth edition of his work, 1889, p. 273).

Homicides sentenced

To penal To Imprisonment Soldiers
servitude

Persons in whom I detected (346) (363) (711) No anomaly in the skull 11.9 p.c. 8.2 p.c. 37.2 p.c. One or two anomalies 47.2 " 56.6 " 51.8 " Three or four anomalies 30.9 " 2.6 " 11 " Five or six anomalies 6.7 " 2.3 " 0 " Seven or more anomalies .3 " .3 " 0 "

That is to say, men with normal skulls were three times as numerous amongst soldiers as they were amongst criminals; of men with a noteworthy number of anomalies occurring together (three or four), there were three times as many amongst criminals as amongst soldiers; and there was not one soldier amongst those who showed an extraordinary number (five or more).

This proves to demonstration not only the greater frequency of anomalous skulls (and the same is true of physiognomical, physiological, and psychological anomalies) amongst criminals, but also that amongst these criminals between fifty and sixty per cent. show very few anomalies, whilst about one-third of the whole number present a remarkable combination, and one-tenth are normal in this respect.

Amongst the statistical data exhibiting the primary characteristics of the majority of criminals, the data connected with relapsed criminals are especially conspicuous. Though relapses, like first offences, are partly due to social conditions, they also have a manifest biological cause, since, under the operation of the same penal system, there are some liberated prisoners who relapse and some who do not.

The statistics of relapse are unfortunately very difficult to collect, on account of differences in the legislation of different countries, and in the preparation of records, which, even under the more general adoption of anthropometrical identification, rarely succeed in preventing the use of fresh names by professional criminals. So that we may still say, in the words of one who is a very good judge in this matter, M. Yvernes, not only that ``the Prisons Congress of London (1872) was compelled to leave various problems undecided for lack of documentary evidence, and especially the question of relapsed criminals," but also that to this day (1879), ``we find varying results in different countries, the exact significance of which is not apparent."

I have, however, published an essay on international statistics of relapsed criminals, from which I drew the following general conclusion: that even in prison statistics, which often give higher totals of relapsed cases than are given by judicial statistics, because they are more personal, and therefore less uncertain, we never obtain the full number of relapses, though the totals given vary from country to country, from district to district, and from prison to prison. It would be impossible to state accurately what proportion the numbers given bear to the actual number; but I am justified in saying, from all the materials which I have collected and compared in the aforesaid essay, that the number of relapses in Europe is generally between 50 and 60 per cent., and certainly rather above than below this limit. Whilst the Italian statistics, for instance, give 14 per cent. of relapses amongst prisoners sentenced to penal servitude, I found by experience 37 per cent; out of 346 who admitted to me that they had relapsed; and, amongst those who had been sentenced to simple imprisonment, I found 60 per cent. out of 363, in place of the 33 per cent. recorded in the prison statistics. The difference may be due to the particular conditions of the prisons which I visited; but in any case it establishes the inadequacy of the official figures dealing with relapse.

After this statement of a general fact, which proves, as Lombroso and Espinas said, that ``the relapsed criminal is the rule rather than the exception," we can proceed to set down the special proportions of relapse for each particular crime, so as to obtain an indication of the forms of crime which are most frequently resorted to by habitual criminals.

For Italy I have found that the highest percentages of relapse are afforded by persons convicted of theft and petty larceny, forgery, rape, manslaughter, conspiracy, and, at the correctional courts, vagrancy and mendacity. The lowest percentages are amongst those convicted of assault and bodily harm, murders, and infanticide.

For France, where legal statistics are remarkably adapted for the most minute inquiry, I have drawn up the following table of statistics from the lists of persons convicted at the assize courts and correctional tribunals, taking an average of the years 1877-81, which is not sensibly affected by the results of succeeding years.

It will be seen that the average of relapses for crimes against the person is higher than the average for the most serious cases of murderous and indecent assault, which are clearly an outcome of the most anti-social tendencies (such as parricide, murder, rape, inflicting bodily harm on parents, &c.). Thus homicide and fatal wounding, though relapse is very frequent in these cases, still display a less abnormal and more occasional character by their lower position in the table, as shown in the cases of infanticide, concealment of birth, and abandonment of infants. As for the very frequent occurrence of relapse in special crimes, such as assaults on officials and resistance to authority, which rarely come before the assize courts--though even there they tend to support the higher numbers in the tribunals--these are offences which may also be committed by criminals of every kind, and which, moreover, depend in some measure on the social factor of police organisation, and frequently on the psycho-pathological state of particular individuals.

The somewhat rare occurrence of relapse in such a grave type of murder as poisoning is noteworthy. But this is only an effect of the special psychology of these criminals, as I have explained elsewhere.

FRANCE--CASES OF RELAPSE, 1877-81. COURTS OF ASSIZE

CRIMES (Against the person) p. 100 Violence against public officers 85.8 Bigamy 59.3 Wounding parents or grandparents 55.9 Riot 55.3 Kidnapping of minors 46.2 Sexual assault on adults 44.0 Wilful murder (assassination) 42.3 Parricide 41.7 Manslaughter (homicide) 39.4 Sexual assaults on children 38.5 Attempts against railways 37.5 Serious wounds followed by death 36.8

General average 35.8

Abortion 30.0 Perjury 26.7 Sequestration 18.8 Poisoning 16.7 Infanticide 6.0 Stealing, substitution or abandoning children 4.9

CRIMES (Against property) p. 100 Theft in churches 74.3 Thefts, simple 71.7 Robbery, with violence, not on the highway 66.0 Burning buildings not inhabited, woods, etc. 59.8

General average 58.5

Barratry 50.0 Theft by servants 44.2 Counterfeiting 43.8 Forgery, private writings 42.5 Burning inhabited dwellings 41.5 Forgery, commercial paper 38.3 Forgery, public documents 37.0 Fraudulent bankruptcy 35.3 Abuse of confidence by domestic servant 32.5 Extortion 30.7 Embezzlement of public funds 28.5 Robbing the mails by postal employees Smuggling by customs officers

CORRECTIONAL TRIBUNALS

DELICTS p. 100

Infractions of surveillance 100 Infractions of expulsion of foreign fugitives 93.0 Infractions of interdiction to sojourn 89.0 Drunkenness 78.4 Vagabondage 71.3 Begging 65.7 Fraud (escroquerie) 47.8 Insult to public officers 46.8 Forcible entry 45.3 Thefts 45.2 Breach of trust 43.8

General average 41.9

Riot, resistance 40.3 Written or verbal threats 39.6 Prohibited weapons, etc.
37.3 Political, electoral, and newspaper delicts 35.7 Outrage to public morality 34.5
Public outrage to decency 32.2 Voluntary wounds and blows 31.0 Unlawful opening
of cafes, inns 27.7 Unlawful practice of medicine or pharmacy 26.6 Contraventions
of railway regulations 25.3 Hunting or carrying prohibited arms 24.2 Breach of good
morals, tending to corruption 23.8 Simple bankruptcy 23.6 Insult to ministers of
religion 20.4 Fraudulent sales of merchandise 16.7 Defamations, insults, calumnies
14.2 Rural delicts 12.0

Amongst crimes against property, the most frequent relapses are found in the
case of thieves (not including thefts and breaches of trust by domestic servants,
which thus, proving their more occasional character, confirm the agreement of
statistics with criminal psychology). The same thing is observed in regard to forgers
of commercial documents and to fraudulent bankrupts, who are partly drawn into
crime under the stress of personal or general crises. And the infrequency of relapse
amongst postal employees condemned for embezzlement, and amongst customs
officers who have been guilty of smuggling, is only a further confirmation of the
inducement to crime by the opportunities met with in each case, rather than by
personal tendencies.

Amongst minor offences, apart from that evasion of supervision which is no
more than a legal condition, there are, both in France and in Italy, very frequent
cases of relapse by vagabonds and mendicants, which is a consequence of social
environment, as well as of the feeble organisation of the individuals. Other relapses
above the average, included amongst these offences, constitute a sort of accessory
criminality, existing side by side with the habitual criminality of thieves, murderers,
and the like, such as drunkenness, attacks on public functionaries, infractions of the
regulations of domicile, &c.

In thefts and resistance to authorities, relapse is less frequent here than in the
assize courts, for in the majority of these minor offences, in their general forms, there
is a greater number of occasional offences, as is also the case with bankruptcies,
defamation, abuse, rural offences, &c., which demonstrate their more occasional
character by their very low figures.

Hence the statistics of general and specific relapse indirectly confirm the fact
that criminals, as a whole, have no uniform anthropological type; and that the bio-
psychical types and anomalies belong more especially to the category of habitual
criminals and those born into the criminal class, who, after all, are the only ones
hitherto studied by criminal anthropologists.

What, then, is the numerical proportion of habitual criminals to the aggregate number of criminals?

In the absence of direct inquiry, it is possible to get at this proportion indirectly, from facts of two kinds. In the first place, a study of the works on criminal anthropology supplies us with an approximate figure, since the biological characteristics united in individuals, in sufficient number to create a criminal type, are met with in between forty and fifty per cent. of the total.

And this conclusion may be confirmed by other data of criminal statistics.

Whilst the statistics of relapse give us a very limited number of crimes and offences committed by born and habitual criminals, science and criminal legislation give us a far more extended classification.

Ellero reckoned in the penal code of the German Empire 203 crimes and offences; and I find that the Italian code of 1859 enumerates about 180, the new code about 200, and the French penal code about 150. Thus the kind of crimes of habitual criminals would only be about one-tenth of the complete legal classification of crimes and offences.

It is easy indeed to suppose that born and habitual criminals do not generally commit political crimes and offences, nor offences connected with the press, nor against freedom of worship, nor in corruption of public functionaries, nor misuse of title or authority; nor calumny, making false attestations or false reports; nor adultery, incest, or abduction of minors; nor infanticide, abortion, or palming of children; nor betrayal of professional secrets; nor bankruptcy offences, nor damage to property, nor violation of domicile, nor illegal arrests, nor duels, nor defamation, nor abuse. I say generally; for, as there are occasional criminals who commit the offences characteristic of habitual criminality, such as homicides, robberies, rapes, &c., so there are born criminals who sometimes commit crimes out of their ordinary course.

It is now necessary to add a few statistical data in respect of the classification of crime, which I take, like the others, from the essay already mentioned.

HABITUAL CRIMINALITY ITALY. FRANCE. BELGIUM. (homicide, theft, conspiracy, rape, incendiarism, vagrancy, swindling) A* B* C* A* B* C* A* B* C* --- Proportion of the persons p.c. p.c. p.c. p.c p.c. p.c. p.c. p.c. p.c. convicted of these crimes and offences to the total number of convictions . . 84 32 38 90 34 35 86 30 30

{* NOTE: A, B and C above are `Assizes,' `Tribunals,' and `Totals,' respectively.}

11

That is to say, habitual criminality would be represented, in Italy, by about 40 per cent. of the total number of condemned persons, and by somewhat less in France and Belgium. This would be accounted for in Belgium by the exclusion of vagrancy; but the difference is virtually due to the greater frequency in Italy of certain crimes, such as homicide, highway robbery with violence, and conspiracies.

Further, it is apparent that in all these countries the types of habitual criminality, with the exception of thefts and vagrancy, are in greater proportion at the assizes, on account of their serious character.

The actual totals, however, are larger at the tribunals, for as, in the scale of animal life, the greatest fecundity belongs to the lower and smaller forms, so in the criminal scale, the less serious offences (such as simple theft, swindling, vagrancy, &c.) are the more numerous. Thus, out of the total of 38 per cent. in Italy, 32 belong to the tribunals and 6 to the assizes; out of 35 per cent in France, 33 belong to the tribunals and 2 to the assizes; and out of 30 per cent. in Belgium, 29 belong to the tribunals and 1 to the assizes. This also is partly accounted for by legislative distinctions as to the respective jurisdictions of these courts.

As to the particulars of the totals, it is found that thefts are the most numerous types in Italy (20 per cent.), in France (24 per cent.), in Belgium (23 per cent.), and in Prussia (37 per cent., including breaches of trust).[5]

[5] Starke, ``Verbrechen und Verbrecher in Preussen," Berlin, 1884, p. 92.

After theft, the most numerous in Italy are vagrancy (5 per cent.), homicides (4 per cent.), swindling (3 per cent.), forgery (.9 per cent.), rape (.4 per cent.), conspiracy (.4 per cent.), and incendiarism (.2 per cent.).

In France and Belgium we find the same relative frequency of vagrancy and swindling; but homicide, incendiarism, and conspiracy are less frequent, whilst rape is more common in France (.5 per cent.) and in Belgium (1 per cent.).

Such then are the most frequent forms of habitual criminality in the generality of condemned persons; and it will be useful now to contrast the more frequent forms of occasional criminality. For Italy the only judicial statistics which are valuable for detailed inquiry are those of 1863, 1869-72. For France, every volume of the admirable series of criminal statistics may be utilised.

It will be seen that the frequency of these occasional crimes and offences in Italy and in France is very variable, though assaults and wounding, resistance to authorities, damage, defamation and abuse, are the most numerous in both countries.

The proportion of each offence to the total also varies considerably, not only through a difference of legislation between Italy and France in regard to poaching, drunkenness, frauds on refreshment-house keepers, and so forth, but also by reason of the different condition of individuals and of society in the two countries. Thus assaults and wounding, which in Italy comprise 23 per cent. of the total of convictions, reach in France no more than 14 per cent., whilst resistance to the authorities, &c., which

YEARLY AVERAGE or CONDEMNED

PERSONS.

ITALY, 1863-72. FRANCE

1877-81 CRIMES AND OFFENCES OF GREATEST

FREQUENCY

(not including those of Habitual Criminals).

p.c. p.c. p.c. p.c.

Wilful Assault and Wounding ... Illegally carrying Arms ...... -- 8 7 -- 3 3 Resistance to Authority, Assaults and

Violence against Public Functionaries ... 3 5 4 --2 10 10

Injury to Property ... ... -- 2 2 -- I 1-6 1 5 Defamation and Abuse ... ... -- s-S 1-6 -- I-6 1 5 Written or Spoken Threats ... ... -- 1 4 1'2 -- '2 --2 Illegal Games ... ... -- I --8 -- 2 1 'I Political Crimes and Offences ...... 31.7 -- --2 -- 4 2 --2 Press Crimes and Offences ... ... 4 4 --4 -- --6 --6 Embezzlement, Corruption, Malfeasance

of Public Functionaries -- --3 .3 -- -- --

Escape from Detention --1 --2 2 -- --6 --6 False Witness .. .. --7 2 --2 09 6 --6 Violation of Domicile ... ... -- 17 .15 -- lo --9 Calumny ... --. --1 I 1 --oS --o8 Exposure, Palming or ``Suppression''

of Infants -- --12 1 --2 --1 --1

Bankruptcy Offences ... ... I 1 --1 1'3 5 --6 Offences against Religion and Ministers

13

of Religion -- 1 --1 -- --7 .07

Duelling ... . -- .04 .03 -- -- -- Abortion ... ... -- -- -- og -- --OI
Offences against the Game Laws -- -- -- -- 13 12-7 Drunkenness -- -- -- -- 1 5 1 5
Offences against Public Decency -- -- -- -- I-8 1.7 Adultery ... ... -- -- -- --5 5
Offences against Morality, with Incitement

to Immorality ... ... -- -- -- -- --2 --2

Involuntary Homicide -- -- -- -- --2 --2

" Wounding -- -- -- -- --6 --6
" Incendiarism -- -- -- -- --2 --2

Illegal Practising of Medicine and

Surgery ... ... -- -- -- -- --2 --2

Frauds on Keepers of Refreshment

Houses ... ... -- -- -- -- I-4 1 4

Rural Offences ... ... -- -- -- -- 6 --6

-- -- m

Yearly Average of Convictions,

Gross Totals 6,273 43,584 49,857 3,300 163,997

167,297

[1] Devastation of crops, destruction of fences. [2] Unauthorised gaming houses;
secret lotteries. [3] An exceptional figure, owing to 528 convictions in 1863, whilst
the average of the other years was nine convictions. [4] Electoral offences.

are 4 per cent. in Italy, touch 9 per cent in France. Sexual crimes and offences
(as we saw in the case of rape), such as abortion, adultery, indecent assaults, and
incitement to immorality, which in Italy present very small and negligible figures, are
more frequent in France. Whilst the illegal carrying of arms, threats, false witness,
escape from detention, violations of domicile, calumny, are of greater frequency in
Italy than in France, the contrary is true of bankruptcy offences, political and press

14

crimes and offences, on account of a manifest difference of the moral, economic, and social conditions of the two countries, which are plainly discernible behind these apparently dry figures.

In addition to this demonstration, we have given anthropological and statistical proofs of the fundamental distinction between habitual and occasional criminals, which had been pointed out by many observers, but which had hitherto remained a simple assertion without manifest consequences.

This same distinction ought to be not only the basis of all sociological theory concerning crime, but also a point of departure for other distinctions more precise and complete, which I set forth in my previous studies on criminals, and which were subsequently reproduced, with more or less of assent, by all criminal sociologists.

In the first place, it is necessary to distinguish, amongst habitual criminals, those who present a conspicuous and clinical form of mental aberration, which accounts for their anti-social activity.

In the second place, amongst habitual criminals who are not of unsound mind, however little the inmates of prisons may have been observed with adequate ideas and experience, there is a clear indication of a class of individuals, physically or mentally abnormal, induced to crime by inborn tendencies, which are manifest from their birth, and accompanied by symptoms of extreme moral insensibility. Side by side with these, another class challenges attention, of individuals who have also been criminals from childhood, and who continue to be so, but who are in a special degree a product of physical and social environment, which has persistently driven them into the criminal life, by their abandonment before and after the first offence, and which, especially in the great towns, is very often forced upon them by the actual incitement of their parents.

Amongst occasional criminals, again, a special category is created by a kind of exaggeration of the characteristics, mainly psychological, of the type itself. In the case of all occasional criminals, the crime is brought about rather by the effects of environment than by the active tendencies of the individual; but whilst in most of these individuals the deciding cause is only a circumstance affecting all alike, with a few it is an exceptional constraint of passion, a sort of psychological tempest, which drives them into crime.

Thus, then, the entire body of criminals may be classed in five categories, which as early as 1880 I described as criminal madmen, born criminals, criminals by contracted habits, occasional criminals, and criminals of passion.

As already observed, criminal anthropology will not finally establish itself until it has been developed by biological, psychological, and statistical monographs on each of these categories, in such a manner as to present their anthropological characteristics with greater precision than they have hitherto attained. So far, observers continue to give us the same characteristics for a large aggregate of criminals, classifying them according to the form of their crime rather than according to their bio-social type. In Lombroso's work, for instance, or in that of Marro (and to some extent even in my work on homicide), the characteristics are stated for a total, or for legal categories of criminals, such as murderers, thieves, forgers, and so on, which include born criminals, occasional and habitual criminals, and madmen. The result is a certain measure of inconsistency, according to the predominance of one type or the other in the aggregate of criminals under observation. This also contributes to render the conclusions of criminal anthropology less evident.

Nevertheless, we may sum up the inquiries which have been made up to the present time; and in particular we may now point out the general characteristics of the five classes of criminals, in accordance with my personal experience in the observation of criminals. It is to be hoped that successive observations of a more methodical kind will gradually reinforce the accuracy of this classification of symptoms.

In the first place, it is evident that in a classification not exclusively biological, if it is to form the anthropological basis of criminal sociology, criminals of unsound mind must in all fairness be included.

The usual objection, recently repeated by M. Joly (``Le Crime,'' p. 62), which holds the term ``criminal madness'' to be self- contradictory, since a madman is not morally responsible, and therefore cannot be a criminal, is not conclusive. We maintain that responsibility to society, the only responsibility common to all criminals, exists also for criminals of unsound mind.

Nor, again, is it correct to say, with M. Bianchi, that mad criminals should be referred to psychiatry, and not to criminal anthropology; for, though psychiatry is concerned with mad criminals in a psycho-pathological sense, this does not prevent criminal anthropology and sociology from also concerning themselves with the same subjects, in order to constitute the natural history of the criminal, and to suggest remedies in the interest of society.

As for criminals of unsound mind, it is necessary to begin by placing in a separate category such as cannot, after the studies of Lombroso and the Italian school of psychiatry, be distinguished from the born criminals properly so-called. These are the persons tainted with a form of insanity which is known under various names, from the ``moral insanity'' of Pritchard to the ``reasoning madness'' of Verga. Moral insanity, illustrated by the works of Mendel, Legrand du Saulle, Maudsley, Krafft-Ebing, Savage, Hugues, Hollander, Tamburini, Bonvecchiato, which, with the lack or atrophy of the moral or social sense, and of APPARENT soundness of mind, is properly speaking only the essential psychological condition of the born criminal.

Beyond these morally insane people, who are very rare--for, as Krafft-Ebing and Lombroso have pointed out, they are found more frequently in prisons than in mad-houses--there is the unhappily large body of persons tainted by a common and clinical form of mental alienation, all of whom are apt to become criminal.

The whole of these criminals of unsound mind cannot be included in a single category; and such, indeed, is the opinion expressed by Lombroso, in the second volume of the fourth edition of his work, after his descriptive analysis of the chief forms of mental alienation. As a matter of fact, not only are the organic, and especially the psychological, characteristics of criminal madmen sometimes identical with and sometimes opposed to those of born and occasional criminals, but these very characteristics vary considerably between the different forms of mental alienation, in spite of the identity of the crime committed.

It is further to be observed, in respect of criminal madmen, that this category also includes all the intermediary types between complete madness and a rational condition, who remain in what Maudsley has called the ``middle zone." The most frequent varieties in the criminality of these partially insane persons, or ``mattoides," are the perpetrators of attacks upon statesmen, who are generally men with a grievance, irascible men, writers of insane documents, and the like, such as Passanante, Guiteau, and Maclean.

In the same category are those who commit terrible crimes without motive, and who nevertheless, according to the complacent psychology of the classical school, would be credited with a maximum of moral soundness.

Again, there are the necrophiles, like Sergeant Bertrand, Verzeni, Menesclou, and very probably the undetected ``Jack the Ripper" of London, who are tainted with a form of sexual psychopathy. Yet again there are such as are tainted with hereditary madness, and especially the epileptics and epileptoids, who may also be assigned to the class of born criminals, according to the plausible hypothesis of Lombroso as to the fundamental identity of congenital criminality, moral madness, and epilepsy. I have always found in my own experience that outrageous murders, not to be explained according to the ordinary psychology of criminals, are accompanied by psychical epilepsy, or larvea.

Born or instinctive criminals are those who most frequently present the organic and psychological characteristics established by criminal anthropology. These are either savage or brutal men, or crafty and idle, who draw no distinction between homicide, robbery or other kinds of crime, and honest industry. ``They are criminals just as others are good workingmen," says Fregier; and, as Romagnosi put it, actual punishment affects them much less than the menace of punishment, or does not affect them at all, since they regard imprisonment as a natural risk of their occupation, as masons regard the fall of a roof, or as miners regard fire-damp. ``They do not suffer in prison. They are like a painter in his studio, dreaming of their next masterpiece. They are on good terms with their gaolers, and even know how to make themselves useful."[5]

[5] Moreau, ``Souvenirs de la petite et grande Roquette," Paris, 1884, ii. 440.

The born criminals and the occasional criminals constitute the majority of the characteristic and diverse types of homicide and thief. Prison governors call them ``gaol-birds." They pass on from the police to the judge and to the prison, and from the prison to the police and to the judge, with a regularity which has not yet impaired the faith of law-makers in the efficacy of punishment as a cure for crime.[6]

[6] Wayland, ``The Incorrigible," in the Journal of Mental Science, 1888. Sichart, ``Criminal Incorrigibles."

No doubt the idea of a born criminal is a direct challenge to the traditional belief that the conduct of every man is the outcome of his free will, or at most of his lack of education rather than of his original physio-psychical constitution. But, in the first place, even public opinion, when not prejudiced in favour of the so-called consequences of irresponsibility, recognises in many familiar and everyday cases that there are criminals who, without being mad, are still not as ordinary men; and the reporters call them ``human tigers," ``brutes," and the like. And in the second place, the scientific proofs of these hereditary tendencies to crime, even apart from the clinical forms of mental alienation, are now so numerous that it is useless to insist upon them further.

The third class is that of the criminals whom, after my prison experience, I have called criminals by contracted habit. These are they who, not presenting the anthropological characteristics of the born criminals, or presenting them but slightly, commit their first crime most commonly in youth, or even in childhood-- almost invariably a crime against property, and far more through moral weakness, induced by circumstances and a corrupting environment, than through inborn and active tendencies. After this, as M. Joly observes, either they are led on by the impunity of their first offences, or, more decisively, prison associations debilitate and corrupt them, morally and physically, the cell degrades them, alcoholism renders them stupid and subject to impulse, and they continually fall back into crime, and become chronically prone to it. And society, which thus abandons them, before and after they leave their prison, to wretchedness, idleness, and temptations, gives them no assistance in their struggle to gain an honest livelihood, even when it does not thrust them back into crime by harassing police regulations, which prevent them from finding or keeping honest employment.[7]

[7] Fliche, ``Comment en devient Criminel,'' Paris, 1886.

Of those criminals who begin by being occasional criminals, and end, after progressive degeneration, by exhibiting the features of the born criminals, Thomas More said, ``What is this but to make thieves for the pleasure of hanging them?'' And it is just this class of criminals whom measures of social prevention might reduce to a minimum, for by abolishing the causes we abolish the effects.

Apart from their organic and psychological characteristics, innate or acquired, there are two bio-sociological symptoms which seem to me to be common, though for distinct reasons, to born criminals and habitual criminals. I mean precocity and relapse. The occasional crime and the crime of passion do not, as a rule, occur before manhood, and rarely or never lead to relapse.

Here are a few figures concerning precocity, derived from international prison statistics:--

PRISONERS UNDER 20 YEARS OF AGE. Male. Female.

p.c. p.c.

Italy (1871--6) ... ... 8.8 6.8 France ('72-5) ... ... 10 7.6 Prussia ('71-7--not over 19 years) ... ... 2.8 2.6 Austria ('72-5) ... ... 9.6 10.6 Hungary ('72-6) ... ... 4.2 9 England ('72-7)--not over 24) ... ... 27.4 14.8 Scotland ('72-7) ... ... 20 7.8 Ireland ('72-7) ... ... 9 3.2 Belgium ('74-5) ... ... 20.8 --- Holland ('72-7) ... ... 22.8 3.7 Sweden ('73-7) ... ... 19.7 17 Switzerland ('74) ... ... 6.6 7 Denmark ('74-5) 9.9 9.6

More recent figures show that the yearly average in France, for 1876-80, out of 4,374 persons brought to trial, was 1 per cent. under sixteen years of age, and 17 per cent. between sixteen and twenty-one; whilst in 1886 the same percentages were .60 and 14. Out of 146,217 accused before the tribunals there were 4 per cent. under sixteen, and 14 per cent. between sixteen and twenty- one. Out of 25,135 females there were 4 per cent. under sixteen, and 11 per cent. between sixteen and twenty-one; whilst in 1886 the percentages were 3 and 14 of males, 2.5 and 14 of females.

In Prussia, of persons accused of crimes and offences in 1860-70, 4 per cent. were under eighteen years.

In Germany, of persons condemned in 1886, 3 per cent. were between twelve and fifteen, 6 per cent. between fifteen and eighteen, and 16 per cent. between eighteen and twenty-one years.

In Italy, out of 5,189 persons condemned at the assizes in 1887, 3 per cent. were between fourteen and eighteen, and 12 per cent. between eighteen and twenty-one. Out of 65,624 tried before the tribunals, 1.2 per cent. were under fourteen, 5 per cent. were between fourteen and eighteen, and 13 per cent. between eighteen and twenty-one. There is a continual increase of precocious criminals in Italy. Prisoners condemned at the assizes under the age of twenty-one stood at 15 per cent. from 1880 to 1887, whilst those of a similar age who were tried before the tribunals rose from 17 to 20 per cent.

To these numerical data may be added others of a qualificative character, showing that precocity is most frequent in respect of the natural crimes and offences which are usually observed amongst born and habitual criminals.

In France the younger prisoners in 1882 had been sentenced in the following proportions:--

Male. Female.

For murder and poisoning ... ... 0.9 per cent. .5 per cent. " homicide, assaults, and wounding 1.6 " 1.5 " " incendiarism... ... ... 1.8 " 2 " " indecent assault ... ... 3.5 " 11.8 " " specified thefts, forgery, uttering

false coin ... ... 5.2 " 2.4 "

" simple theft, swindling ... 60.8 " 49.7 " " mendacity and vagrancy ... 23 " 20.5 " " other crimes and offences ... 2.7 " 8 " " defiance of parents ... ... 1 " 10.5 "

These figures, showing a greater frequency amongst females of precocious crimes against the person, and amongst males against property, are approximately repeated in Switzerland, where young prisoners in 1870-74 had been sentenced in these proportions:--

For crimes and offences against the person ... 12.1 per cent. " " " morality ... 5.7 " " incendiarism... ... ... 4.3 " " theft ... ... 65.5 " " swindling ... ... 5.4 " " forgery ... ... 1.9 " " vagrancy ... ... 4.6 "

The judicial statistics of France and Italy give these proportions:--

{FIX THIS TABLE!}

ITALY--1866. FRANCE--1886

ASSIZE COURTS Under 14--18. 28--21. Under j l6--2

Homicide ... ... p.c. p.c. p.c. p.c. p.c. Murder(and robbery with homicide) 14 1 i 10 3 7 6 Parricide .... -- 5 --8 7 5 9 Infanticide ... ... -- 1 --4 -- 6 Imprisonment ... ... -- -- -- Wilful wounding (followed by death) -- 19 24 -- 3 S Abortion .... -- -- -- 1-1 Rape and indecent assault on adults}-- 1'2

" " children}-- 10 7 t 3 7 11

Resistance to and attacks on public

functionaries ... ... -- 5 --6 -- 3

Incendiarism -- -- --2 3-7 3 1 False money ... . 14 -- 1 3-7 2 5 Forgery in public and private docu-

ments .... -- 5 --2 -- 2 --1

Extortion, highway robbery with

violence ... ... 14 9 7 -- 3w 6

Specified and simple theft ... 14 19 16 41 51 Unintentional wounding ... 28 5 2 -- -- --- Total of condemned and accused 7 179 475 27 641

The French statistics for the tribunals--no complete Italian statistics being available, are as follows:--

FRANCE--1886. CORRECTIONAL TRIBUNALS.

le. Female. Offences. Under 16. 16--21 Under 16.1 16--21

per cent. per cent. per cent. per cent.

Resistance to authorities ... ... 2 2 2 '1 1 1 Assaults on public functionaries --8 5 --7 4 1 Vagrancy ... .-- 4 4 11 2 3 2 S'S Mendacity ... ... 4 8 4 12'- 3 6 Wilful wounding ... ... 5 1 18-5 300 11 Unintentional wounding ... 8 7 1

21

Offences against public decency .. 1 6 1 8 3 1 3 Defamation and abuse - 1 '2 1 1 1 0 Theft ... ... 57 5 a--4 63 54 3 Frauds on refreshment-house keepers --1 2 1 --1 6 Swindling 5 1 2 2.4 3 +2 Breach of confidence ... ... 9 1 3 7 1 2 Injury to crops and plants ... 5 --3 --3 5 Game-law offences .. ... .-- 15 1 14 2 1 1 --2 --- Total of accused

Here we have a statistical demonstration of a more frequent precocity, amongst various forms of criminality, in respect of inborn tendencies (murder and homicide, rape, incendiarism, specific thefts), or in respect of tendencies contracted by habit (simple theft, mendacity, vagrancy).

Also this characteristic of precocity is accompanied by that of relapse, which accordingly we have seen to be more frequent in the same forms of natural criminality, and which we can now tabulate in respect of its persistency in these born and habitual criminals.

It has been well said that the large number of relapsed persons who are brought to trial year after year proves that thieves ply their trade as a regular calling; the thief who has once tasted prison life is sure to return to it.[8] And again, there are very few cases in which a man or a woman who has turned thief ceases to be one. Whatever the reason may be, as a matter of fact the thief is rarely or never reformed. When you can turn an old thief into an honest worker, you may turn an old fox into a house dog.[9]

[8] Quarterly Review, 1871, ``The London Police." [9] Thomson, ``The Psychology of Criminals," Journal of Mental Science, 1870.

We must, however, read these testimonies of practical men, which could easily be multiplied, in the light of our distinction between incorrigible criminals, who are so from their birth, and such as are made incorrigible by the effect of their prison and social environment. The former could scarcely be reduced in number, whilst the latter could be considerably diminished by the penal alternatives of which I will speak later.

The following statistics of relapse are quoted from Yvernes, ``La Recidive en Europe" (Paris, 1874):--

FRANCE--1826-74.

ITALY--1870. Relapses ENGLAND--1871. SWEDEN--1871. Accused Accused

Prisoners. Thieves. and brought and brought
to trial. to trial.

Once ... ... 38 per cent. 54 per cent. 45 per cent. 60 per cent. Twice ... 18 " 28 " 20 " 30 " Three times... 44 " 18 " 35 " 10 "

In Prussia (1878-82), 17 per cent. had relapsed once, 16 per cent. twice, 16 per cent. three times, 13 per cent. four times, 10 per cent five times, and 28 per cent. six times or oftener.[10]

[10] Starke, ``Verbrechen und Verbrecher,'' Berlin, 1884, p. 229.

At the Prisons Congress of Stockholm the following figures were given for Scotland. Out of a total of forty-nine relapsed prisoners, 16 per cent. had relapsed once, 13 per cent. twice or three times, 6 per cent. four or five times, 6 per cent. from six to ten times, 5 per cent. from ten to twenty times, 4 per cent. from twenty to fifty times, and 1 per cent. more than fifty times.

At the meeting of the Social Science Congress, held at Liverpool, in 1876, Mr. Nugent stated that upwards of 4,107 women had relapsed four times or oftener, and that many of them were classed as incorrigible, having been convicted twenty; forty, or fifty times, whilst one had been convicted 130 times.

The judicial statistics of Italy for 1887 give the following results:--

ITALY--Convicted, per cent. Relapses.
Justices of Tribunals. Assizes.
Peace.

Once ... ... 57 42 50 Two to five times ... 34 40 40 More than five times ... 9 18 10 --- Actual totals of relapses 27,068 16,240 1,870

I have found from my inquiries amongst 346 condemned to penal servitude and 353 prisoners from the correctional tribunals the following percentages:--

Relapsed. Convicts Imprisoned. Once ... ... 83.2 ... ... 26 Twice ... ... 12.5 ... ... 16.5 3 times ... ... 3.1 ... ... 14.6 4 " ... ... -- ... ... 10.8 5 " ... ... 6.8 ... ... 6.6 6 " ... ... -- ... ... 5.2 7 " ... ... 1.6 ... ... 7.1 8 " ... ... -- ... ... 2.8 9 " ... ... -- ... ... 2.8 10 " ... ... -- ... ... 2.3 11 " ... ... -- ... ... .9 12 " ... ... -- ... ... .5 13 " ... ... -- ... ... .9 14 " ... ... -- ... ... 1.4 15 " ... ... -- ... ... .9 20 " ... ... -- ... ... .5 -- Actual totals of relapses 128 212

Chronic relapse is naturally less frequent in the case of those condemned to long terms; but it is a conspicuous symptom of individual and social pathology in the two classes of born and habitual criminals.

Lombroso, in the second volume of his work on ``The Criminal,'' denies that precocity and relapse are characteristics distinguishing born and habitual from occasional criminals. But it is only a question of terms. He considers that born and habitual criminals confine themselves almost exclusively to serious crime, and occasional criminals to minor offences. And as the figures which I have given show that precocity and relapse are even more frequent for minor offences than for crimes, he thinks that they contradict instead of confirming my conclusions.

The mere seriousness of an act cannot by any means divide the categories of criminals; for homicide as well as theft, assault and battery as well as forgery, may be committed, though in different psychological and social conditions, as easily by born and habitual criminals as by occasional criminals and criminals of passion.

Moreover, the figures which I have given show that precocity and relapse are more frequent in the forms of criminality which, apart from their gravity, are the common practices of born and habitual criminals, such as murder, homicide, robbery, rape, &c., whilst they are far more uncommon, even if they can be said to be observed at all, in the case of the crimes and offences usually committed by occasional criminals, such as infanticide, and certain of the offences mentioned above.

It remains to say something of the occasional criminals, and the criminals of passion.

The latter are but a variety of the occasional criminals, but their characteristics are so specific that they may be very readily distinguished. In fact Lombroso, in his second edition, supplementing the observations of Despine and Bittinger, separated them from other criminals, and classified them according to their symptoms. I need only summarise his observations.

In the first place, the criminals who constitute the strongly marked class of criminals by irresistible impulse are very rare, and their crimes are almost invariably against the person. Thus, out of 71 criminals of passion inquired into by Lombroso, 69 were homicides, 6 had in addition been convicted of theft, 3 of incendiarism, and 1 of rape.

It may be shown that they number about 5 per cent. of crimes against the person.

They are as a rule persons of previous good behaviour, sanguine or nervous by temperament, of excessive sensibility, unlike born or habitual criminals, and they are often of a neurotic or epileptoid temperament, of which their crimes may be, strictly speaking, an unrecognised consequence.

Frequently they transgress in their youth, especially in the case of women, under stress of a passion which suddenly spurns constraint, like anger, or outraged love, or injured honour. They are highly emotional before, during, or after the crime, which they do not commit treacherously, but openly, and often by ill-chosen methods, the first that present themselves. Now and then, however, one encounters criminals of passion who premeditate a crime, and carry it out treacherously, either by reason of their colder and less impulsive temperament, or as the outcome of preconceived ideas or a widespread sentiment, in cases where we have to do with a popular form of lawlessness, such as the vendetta.

This is why the test of premeditation has no absolute value in criminal psychology, as a distinction between the born criminal and the criminal of passion; for premeditation depends especially on the temperament of the individual, and is exemplified in crimes committed by both anthropological types.

Amongst other symptoms of the criminal of passion, there is also the precise motive which leads to a crime complete in itself, and never as a means of attaining another criminal purpose.

These offenders immediately acknowledge their crime, with unassumed remorse, frequently so keen that they instantly commit, or attempt to commit suicide. When convicted--as they seldom are by a jury--they are always repentant prisoners, and amend their lives, or do not become degraded, so that in this way they encourage superficial observers to affirm as a general fact, and one possible in all circumstances, that ameliorative effect of imprisonment which is really a mere illusion in the case of the far more numerous classes of born and habitual criminals.

In these same offenders we very rarely observe, if at all, the organic anomalies which create a criminal type. And even the psychological characteristics are much slighter in countries where certain crimes of passion are endemic, almost ranking amongst the customs of the community, like the homicides which occur in Corsica and Sardinia for the vindication of honour, or the political assassinations in Russia and Ireland.

The last class is that of occasional criminals, who without any inborn and active tendency to crime lapse into crime at an early age through the temptation of their personal condition, and of their physical and social environment, and who do not lapse into it, or do not relapse, if these temptations disappear.

Thus they commit those crimes and offences which do not indicate natural criminality, or else crimes and offences against person or property, but under personal and social conditions altogether different from those in which they are committed by born and habitual criminals.

25

There is no doubt that, even with the occasional criminal, some of the causes which lead him into crime belong to the anthropological class; for external causes would not suffice without individual predispositions. For instance, during a scarcity or a hard winter, not all of those who experience privation have recourse to theft, but some prefer to endure want, however undeserved, without ceasing to be honest, whilst others are at the utmost driven to beg their food; and amongst those who yield to the suggestion of crime, some stop short at simple theft, whilst others go as far as robbery with violence.

But the true difference between the born and the occasional criminal is that, with the former, the external cause is less operative than the internal tendency, because this tendency possesses, as it were, a centrifugal force, driving the individual to commit crime, whilst, for the occasional criminal, it is rather a case of feeble power of resistance against external causes, to which most of the inducement to crime is due.

The casual provocation of crime in the born criminal is generally the outcome of an instinct or tendency already existing, and far more of a pretext than an occasion of crime. With the occasional criminal, on the other hand, it is the casual provocation which matures, no doubt in a favouring soil, the growth of criminal tendencies not previously developed.

For this reason Lombroso calls the occasional criminals ``criminaloids," in order to show precisely that they have a distinctly abnormal constitution, though in a less degree than the born criminals, just as we have the metal and the metalloid, the epileptic and the epileptoid.

And this, again, is the reason why Lombroso's criticisms on my description of occasional criminals are lacking in force. He says, as Benedikt said at the Congress at Rome, that all criminals are criminals by birth, so that there is no such thing as an occasional criminal, in the sense of a NORMAL individual casually launched into crime. But I have not, any more than Garofalo, drawn such a picture of the occasional criminal, for as a matter of fact I have said precisely the opposite, as indeed Lombroso himself acknowledges a little further on (ii. 422), namely, that between the born and the occasional criminal there is only a difference of degree and modality, as in all the criminal classes.

To cite a few details of criminal psychology, it may be stated that of the two physiological conditions of crime, moral insensibility and improvidence, occasional crime is especially due to the latter, and inborn and habitual crime to the former. With the born criminal it is, above all, the lack or the weakness of moral sense which fails to withstand crime, whereas with the occasional criminal the moral sense is almost normal, but inability to realise beforehand the consequences of his act causes him to yield to external influences.

Every man, however pure and honest he may be, is conscious now and then of a transitory notion of some dishonest or criminal action. But with the honest man, exactly because he is physically and morally normal, this notion of crime, which simultaneously summons up the idea of its grievous consequences, glances off the surface of the normal conscience, and is a mere flash without the thunder. With the man who is less normal and has less forethought, the notion dwells, resists the weak repulsion of a not too vigorous moral sense, and finally prevails; for, as Victor Hugo says, ``Face to face with duty, to hesitate is to be lost."[11]

[11] For instance, I will recall a fact which Morel has related of himself, how one day, as he was crossing a bridge in Paris, he saw a working-man gazing into the water, and a homicidal idea flashed across his mind, so that he had to hurry away, for fear of yielding to the temptation to throw the man into the water. Again, there is the case of Humboldt's nurse, who was attacked one day by the temptation to kill her charge, and ran with him to his mother in order to avoid a disaster. Brierre de Boismont also tells us of a learned man who, at the sight of a picture in a public gallery, was tempted to cut the canvas, and ran away from his impulse to crime.

The criminal of passion is one who is strong enough to resist ordinary temptations of no exceptional force, to which the occasional criminal would yield, but who does not resist psychological storms which indeed are sometimes actually irresistible.

The forms of occasional criminality, which are determined by these ordinary temptations, are also determined by age, sex, poverty, worldly influences, influences of moral environment, alcoholism, personal surroundings, and imitation. Tarde has ably demonstrated the persistent influence of these conditions on the actions of men.

In this connection, Lombroso has drawn a clear distinction between two varieties of occasional criminals: the ``pseudo-criminals," or normal human beings who commit involuntary offences, or offences which do not spring from perversity, and do not hurt society, though they are punishable by law, and ``criminaloids," who commit ordinary offences, but differ from true criminals for the reasons already given.

A final observation is necessary in regard to this anthropological classification of criminals, and it meets various objections raised by our syllogistic critics. The difference existing amongst the five categories is only one of degree, and depends upon their organic and psychological types, and upon the influence of physical and social environment.

In every natural classification the differences between various groups and varieties are never anything but relative. This deprives them of none of their theoretical and practical importance, and so it is with this anthropological classification of criminals.

It follows that, as in natural history we advance by degrees and shades from the inorganic to the organic creation, life beginning in the mineral domain with the laws of crystallisation, so in criminal anthropology we pass by degrees and shades from the mad to the born criminal, through the links of moral madmen and epileptics; and from the born criminal to the occasional, through the link of the habitual criminal, who begins by being an occasional criminal, and ends by acquiring and transmitting to his children the characteristics of the born criminal. And finally, we pass from the occasional criminal to the criminal of passion, who is but a species of the other, and who further, with his neurotic and epileptoid temperament, not infrequently approximates to the criminal of unsound mind.

Thus in our everyday life, as in science, we very often find intermediate types, for complete and unmixed types are always the most uncommon. And whilst legislators and judges, in their complacent psychology, exact and establish marked lines of cleavage between the sane and the insane criminal, experts in psychiatry and anthropology are often constrained to place a prisoner somewhere between the mad and the born criminal, or between the occasional criminal and the normal man.

But it is evident that even when a criminal cannot be classed precisely in one or the other category, and stands between the two, this is in itself a sufficiently definite classification, especially from a sociological point of view. There is consequently no weight in the objection of those who, basing their argument on an abstract and nebulous idea of the criminal in general, and judging him merely according to the crime which has been committed, without knowing his personal characteristics and the circumstances of his environment, affirm that criminal anthropology cannot classify all who are detained and accused.

In my experience, however, as a counsel and as an observer, I have never had any difficulty in classifying all persons detained or condemned for crimes and offences, by relying upon organic, and especially upon psychological symptoms.

Thus, as Garofalo recently said, whilst the accepted criminal science recognises only two terms, the offence and the punishment, criminal sociology on the other hand recognises three: the crime, the criminal, and the means best calculated for social self- defence. And it may be concluded that up to this time, science, legislation, and, in a minor degree, but without any scientific method, the administration of justice, have judged and punished crime in the person of the criminal, but that hereafter it will be necessary to judge the criminal as well as the crime.

After these general observations on the anthropological classes of criminals, it might seem necessary to establish their respective numerical proportions. But as there is no absolute separation between one and another, and as the frequency of the several criminal types varies according to the crimes or offences, natural or otherwise, against persons or property, no precise account can be rendered of the criminal world as a whole.

By way of approximation, however, it may be said in the first place that the classes of mad criminals and criminals of passion are the least numerous, and represent something like 5 or 10 per cent. of the total.

On the other hand, we have seen that born and habitual criminals are about 40 or 50 per cent.; so that the occasional criminals would also be between 40 and 50 per cent.

These are figures which naturally vary according to the different groups of crime and of criminals which come under observation, and which cannot be more accurately determined without a series of special studies in criminal anthropology, as I said when answering the objections which have been raised against the methods of this novel science.

It remains for us, before concluding our first chapter, to establish a fact of great scientific and practical value. This is that, after the anthropological classification which I have maintained for some ten years past, all who have been devoting themselves to the subject of crime as regarded from a biological and social standpoint have recognised the need for a classification less simple than that of habitual and occasional criminals, and which will be more or less complex according to the criterion which may be adopted.

In the first place, the necessity is generally recognised of abandoning the old arbitrary and algebraic type in favour of a classification which shall correspond more accurately with the facts of the case. This classification, originating in observations made within the prison walls, I have extended in the domain of criminal sociology, wherein it is now established as a fundamental criterion of legislative measures which must be taken as a protection against criminals, as well as a criterion of their responsibility.

Secondly, the classifications of criminals hitherto given are not essentially and integrally distinct. It has been seen, as a matter of fact, that all the classifications which have been set forth amount to a recognition of four types, the born, the insane, the occasional criminals, and the criminals of passion; and this again resolves itself into the simple and primitive distinction between occasional and instinctive criminals. The category of criminals by contracted habit would not be accepted by all observers, but it corresponds too closely to our daily experience to stand in need of further proof. And on the other hand I must frankly decline to accept the authority of those who put forward classifications more or less symmetrical without having made a direct study of criminals; for the experimental method does not admit systems based on mere imagination, or on vague recollections of criminal trials, or on argumentative constructions built up from the systems of others.

As a matter of fact, apart from the differences of nomenclature, it is evident that the partial discrepancies in this anthropological classification of criminals are due in some measure to the different points of view taken by observers. For instance, the classification of Lacassagne, Joly, Krauss, Badik, and Marro rest upon a purely descriptive criterion of the organic or psychological characteristics of criminals. The classifications of Liszt, Medem, and Minzloff, on the other hand, depend solely upon the curative and defensive influence of punishment; and those of Foehring and Starke upon certain special points of view, such as the assistance of released prisoners, on their tendency to relapse.

My own point of view, on the contrary, has been general and reproductive, for my classification is based upon the natural causes of crime, individual, physical, and social, and to this extent it corresponds more closely with the theoretical and practical requirements of criminal sociology. If the curative art of society, like that of individuals, expects from positive knowledge an indication of remedies, it is clear that a classification based on the fundamental causes of crime is best fitted to indicate a social cure for this manifestation of disease, which is the essential object of criminal sociology. For, as in biology one is carried from purely descriptive anatomy to genetic anatomy and physiology, so in sociology we must pass on from purely legal descriptions of crimes to the genetic knowledge of the criminals who commit these crimes.

For this reason all the chief classifications of criminals, as has been seen, may be brought into line with my own, by virtue of the more complete and fruitful test which has established it. And thus we have a manifest proof that this classification actually represents the common and permanent basis of all the chief anthropological categories of criminals, whether in regard to their natural causality and their specific character, or in regard to the different forms of social self-defence which spring out of them, and which must be adapted to the natural causes of crime, and to the principal criminal types.

But whatever classification may be accepted, we shall always have, as the fundamental axiom of criminal anthropology, this variety in the types of criminals, which must henceforth be indispensable to all who are theoretically or practically concerned with crime.

CHAPTER II.

THE DATA OF CRIMINAL STATISTICS.

For moral and social facts, unlike physical and biological facts, experiment is very difficult, and frequently even impossible; observation in this domain brings the greatest aid to scientific research. And statistics are amongst the most efficacious instruments of such observation.

It is natural, therefore, that criminal sociology, after studying the individual aspect of the natural genesis of crime, should have recourse to criminal statistics for the study of the social aspect. Statistical information in the words of Krohne, ``is the first condition of success in opposing the armies of crime, for it discharges the same function as the Intelligence department in war."

From statistics, in fact, the modern idea of the close relation between offences and the conditions of social life, in some of its aspects, and above all in certain particular forms, has most directly sprung.

The science of criminal statistics is to criminal sociology what histology is to biology, for it exhibits, in the conditions of the individual elements of the collective organism, the factors of crime as a social phenomenon. And that not only for scientific inductions, but also for practical and legislative purposes; for, as Lord Brougham said at the London Statistical Congress in 1860, ``criminal statistics are for the legislator what the chart and the compass are for the navigator."

The experimental school, accepting the fundamental and incontestible idea, apart from its numerical and optimistic exaggerations, that the statistics of crime must be considered in regard to the growth and activity of the population, has opened up an entirely new channel of fruitful observations, in the classification and study of the natural factors of crime.

In my ``Studies of Crime in France" (1881) I arranged in three natural orders the whole series of causes leading to crime, which had previously been indicated in a fragmentary and incomplete manner.[12]

[12] Bentham, in his ``Introduction to the Principles of Morals and Legislation," enumerates the following circumstances as necessary to be considered in legislation:--temperament, health, strength, physical imperfections, culture, intellectual faculties, strength of mind, dispositions, ideas of honour and religion,

31

feelings of sympathy and antipathy, insanity, economic conditions, sex, age, social status, education, profession, climate, race, government, religious profession.

Lombroso, in the second edition of his ``Criminal,'' which embraces all the divisions of his classical work, has made but a rapid enumeration of the principal points:--race civilisation, poverty, heredity, age sex, civil status, profession, education, organic anomalies, sensations imitation. Morselli, treating of suicide, has given a fuller classification of its contributory causes:--worldly or natural influences, ethnical or demographical influences, social influences, biopsychical influences.

From the consideration that human actions, whether honest or dishonest, social or anti-social, are always the outcome of a man's physio-psychical organism, and of the physical and social atmosphere which surrounds him, I have drawn attention to the anthropological or individual factors of crime, the physical factors, and the social factors.

The anthropological factors, inherent in the individual criminal, are the first condition of crime; and they may be divided into three sub-classes, according as we regard the criminal organically physically, or socially.

The organic constitution of the criminal comprises all anomalies of the skull, the brain, the vital organs, the sensibility, and the reflex activity, and all the bodily characteristics taken together, such as the physiognomy, tattooing, and so on.

The mental constitution of the criminal comprises anomalies of intelligence and feeling, especially of the moral sense, and the specialities of criminal writing and slang.

The personal characteristics of the criminal comprise his purely biological conditions, such as race, age, sex; bio-social conditions, such as civil status, profession, domicile, social rank, instruction, education, which have hitherto been regarded as almost the exclusive concern of criminal statistics.

The physical factors of crime are climate, the nature of the soil, the relative length of day and night, the seasons, the average temperature, meteoric conditions, agricultural pursuits.

The social factors comprise the density of population; public opinion, manners and religion; family circumstances; the system of education; industrial pursuits; alcoholism; economic and political conditions; public administration, justice and police; and in general, legislative, civil and penal institutions. We have here a host of latent causes, commingling and combining in all parts of the social organism, which generally escape the notice both of theorists and of practical men, of criminologists and of legislators.

This classification of the natural factors of crime, which has indeed been accepted by almost all criminal anthropologists and sociologists, seems to me more precise and complete than any other which has been proposed.

In respect of this classification of the natural factors of crime, it is necessary to make two final observations as to the practical results which may be obtained in the struggle for just laws and against the transgression of them.

In the first place, owing to ``the discovery of the unexpected relation amongst the various forces of nature, which had previously been thought to be independent,'' we must lay stress on this positive deduction, that we cannot find an adequate reason either for a single crime or for the aggregate criminality of a nation if we do not take into account each and all of the different natural factors, which we may isolate in the exigencies of our studies, but which always act together in an indissoluble union.

No crime, whoever commits it, and in whatever circumstances, can be explained except as the outcome of individual free-will, or as the natural effect of natural causes. Since the former of these explanations has no scientific value, it is impossible to give a scientific explanation of a crime (or indeed of any other action of man or brute) unless it is considered as the product of a particular organic and psychical constitution, acting in a particular physical and social environment.

Therefore it is far from being exact to assert that the positive criminal school reduces crime to a purely and exclusively anthropological phenomenon. As a matter of fact, this school has always from the beginning maintained that crime is the effect of anthropological, physical, and social conditions, which evolve it by their simultaneous and inseparable operation. And if inquiries into biological conditions have been more abundant and more conspicuous by their novelty, this in no way contradicts the fundamental conclusion of criminal sociology.

That being stated, we have still to examine the relative value of these three classes of conditions in the natural evolution of crime.

It seems to me that this question is generally stated inaccurately, and also that it cannot be answered absolutely, and in a word.

It is generally stated inaccurately; because they who think, for instance, that crime is nothing else than a purely and exclusively social phenomenon in the evolution of which the organic and psychical anomalies of the criminal have had no part, ignore more or less consciously the universal correlation of natural forces, and forget that, in regard to any phenomenon whatsoever, it is impossible to set an absolute limit to the network of its causes, immediate and remote, direct and indirect.

To put this question in an arbitrary sense would be like asking if a mammal is the product of its lungs, or its heart, or its stomach, or of vegetable constituents, or of the atmosphere; whereas each of these conditions, internal and external, is necessary to the life of the animal.

In fact, if crime were the exclusive product of the social environment, how could one explain the familiar fact that in the same social environment, and in identical circumstances of poverty, abandonment, lack of education, sixty per cent. do not commit crimes, and, of the other forty, five prefer suicide, five go mad, five simply become beggars or tramps not dangerous to society, whilst the remaining twenty-five actually commit crimes? And amongst the latter, whilst some go no further than theft without violence, why do others commit theft with violence, and even kill their victim outright, before he offers resistance, or threatens them, or calls for help, and this with no other object than gain?

The secondary differences of social condition, which may be observed even amongst the members of a single family, rotting in one of the slums of our great towns, or amongst those who are surrounded by the temptations of money or power, or the like, are clearly not enough in themselves to explain the vast differences in the actions which grow out of them, varying from honesty under the greatest discouragement to suicide and murder.

The question, therefore, must be asked in a relative sense altogether, and we must inquire which of the three kinds of natural causes of crime has a greater or less influence in determining each particular crime at any given moment in the individual and social life.

No clear answer of general application can be given to this question, for the relative influence of the anthropological, physical, and social conditions varies with the psychological and social characteristics of each offence against the law.

For instance, if we consider the three great classes of crimes against the person, against property, and against personal purity, it is evident that each class of determining causes, but especially the biological and social conditions, have a distinctly different influence in evolving homicide, theft, or indecent assaults. And so it is in every category of crimes.

The undeniable influence of social conditions, and still more of economic conditions, in leading up to the commission of theft, is far inferior in the genesis of homicides and indecent assaults. And similarly, in each category of crimes, the influence of the determining conditions varies greatly according to the special forms of crime.

Certain casual homicides are plainly the result of social conditions (gambling, drink, public opinion, &c.) in a much higher degree than homicides which for the most part spring from brutality, from the moral insensibility of individuals, or from their psycho-pathological conditions, corresponding to abnormal organic conditions.

In like manner, certain indecent assaults, incests, &c., are largely the outcome of social environment, which, condemning a number of persons to live in hovels without air or light, with a promiscuity of sex between parents and children such as obtains amongst the brutes, effaces or deadens all normal sense of modesty. On the other hand, there are cases of rape and the like which are mostly due to the biological condition of the individual, either in manifest forms of sexual disease or, less manifest though none the less actual, of biological anomaly.

For thefts, again, whilst occasional simple thefts are largely the effect of social and economical conditions, this influence becomes feebler in comparison with impulses due to the personal constitution, organic and psychical, as, for instance, in the case of thefts with violence, and especially of murder for the purpose of robbery, which scoundrels of the ''swell-mob" so frequently commit in cold blood.

The same observation applies to the conditions of physical environment. For instance, if the regular increase of crimes against property in winter (and, as I showed for the first time from French statistics, in years when the cold is greatest) is only an indirect result, through the social and economic influences of temperature, the increase of crimes of passion and indecent assaults during the months and years when the temperature is highest is only a direct effect of temperature, even for such as, by their biological conditions, offer the feeblest resistance to these influences.

Meanwhile, a last objection has been raised against the conclusions which I have maintained for many years past.

It has been said that, even if we admit that for certain crimes and criminals the greatest influence must be recognised as due to the physical and psychical conditions of the individual, extending from slightly manifested anomalies of an anthropological character to the most accentuated pathological condition, this does not exclude the possibility of a crime being due to social conditions. In fact, it is said the anomalies of the individual are in their turn only an effect of a debasing social environment, which condemns its victims to organic and psychical degeneration.

This objection is sound enough if it be taken in a relative sense, but groundless if it be insisted on absolutely.

It must be considered, in the first place, that the distinctions of cause and effect are only relative, for every effect has its cause, and vice versa; so that if wretchedness, material and moral, is a cause of degeneration, degeneration itself, like

35

biological anomaly, is a cause of wretchedness. And in this sense the question would be simply metaphysical, like the famous Byzantine discussions as to whether there was originally an egg before a hen or a hen before an egg.

And, in fact, when it was said, in regard to criminal geography, that the extent and quality of crime in such and such a province, instead of being the effect of biological conditions (race, &c.) and physical conditions (climate, soil, &c.), were but the effect of social and economic conditions (of rural and industrial pursuits, and the like), I was able to make a very simple reply. For, apart even from statistical proofs, if the social conditions of such and such a province, which have an unquestionable influence, are really the absolute and exclusive cause of crime, we may still ask whether these social conditions of the province are not themselves the effect of the ethnical qualities of energy, intelligence, and so forth, in its inhabitants, and of the more or less favourable conditions of the climate and the soil.

But it may also be observed, more precisely, that even apart from strongly marked and conspicuous pathological conditions, which meanwhile assert themselves amongst the biological factors of crime, there is a very great number of these cases in which it cannot actually be said that the bio-psychical anomalies of the criminal are the effect of a physically and morally poisonous environment.

In every family in which there are several children, we find (in spite of identical surroundings and conditions of a favourable kind, and suitable methods of training and education), individuals who differ intellectually from the cradle; we also find in the degree or in the kind of their talent, the same individuals also differ from their cradle in physical and moral constitution. And though the phenomenon may only be manifest in the less numerous cases of types which are markedly normal or abnormal, it is none the less true also in the more numerous cases of ordinary types.

In this connection I may observe that physical and social conditions have a greater or a less influence in proportion as the physical and psychical constitution of the individual is more or less sound and vigorous.

The practical conclusion, therefore, of these general observations on the natural genesis of crime is this: Every crime is the result of individual physical and social conditions; and, since these conditions have a more or less dominant influence for various forms of crime, the most certain and profitable mode of defence which society can employ against criminality is of a twofold character, and both modes ought to be employed and brought into action simultaneously--in the first place, the amelioration of the social conditions, as a natural preventive of crime, in the nature of a substitute for punishment; and, secondly, measures of perpetual or temporary elimination of criminals, according as the influence of biological conditions in the evolution of crime is all but absolute, or more or less great, and more or less curable.

As a matter of fact, when we follow the periodic variations of crime, with its measured growth and decrease, we cannot fail to conclude that these constant and constantly occurring variations depend upon a corresponding variation of anthropological and physical factors. For, whilst criminal statistics are far from showing the regularity which Quetelet claimed with much exaggeration, the proportional figures in regard to the bearings of age, sex, calling, &c., upon criminality exhibit very insignificant variations from year to year. And as for the physical factors, if marked variations are explicable at some given period, it is nevertheless evident that neither climate, nor the nature of the soil, nor atmospheric conditions, nor the seasons, nor the temperature of different years could have undergone in the last half-century such constant and repeated variations as to correspond to those waves of criminality which we shall presently exhibit in almost every nation of Europe.

Thus it is to the social factors that we must chiefly attribute the periodic variations of criminality. For even the variations which can be detected in certain anthropological factors, like the influences of age and sex upon crime, and the more or less marked outbreak of anti-social and pathological tendencies, depend in their turn upon social factors, such as the protection accorded to abandoned infants, the participation of women in non-domestic, commercial and industrial life, preventive and repressive measures, and the like. And again, since the social factors have special import in occasional crime, and crime by acquired habit, and since these are the most numerous sections of crime as a whole, it is clear that the periodic movement of crime must be attributed in the main to the social factors. So true is this, that, as we shall presently see, the gravest crimes, especially against persons, precisely because they mostly indicate congenital criminality, follow a more steady and regular movement than these slighter but far more frequent offences against property, public order, and persons, of a more occasional character, and that, as microbes of the world of crime, they are the more direct outcome of social environment.

It is therefore another point in favour of the experimental school that it has insisted on this sociological aspect of the problem of criminality, by showing legislators, outside the limits of their punitive remedies, as easy as they are illusory, how they might, as far as circumstances will permit, apply a genuine social remedy to crime.

After these preliminary observations, it is time that we should take a closer view of the general statistics of the movement of crime in Europe, so far as they may be followed in official figures.

Whilst we have no intention of offering a body of comparative statistics, but only of giving a simple indication of the periodic movement of crime, these data, which do not render it easy to compare one country with another, though they are intimately related so far as each particular country is concerned, suffice to exhibit a few facts of some considerable importance.

The most conspicuous general phenomenon in the countries here included is the steadiness of the gravest forms of crime side by side with the continuous increase of slighter offences, especially in the countries which show a long series of figures, such as France, England, and Belgium. This proceeds mainly from the progressive accumulation of offences against special enactments, which are constantly being added to the original basis of the penal code; but it is also a symptom of an actual transformation in the criminal activity of the century, from whence, through the gradual substitution of crimes against property in the great towns for crimes against the person in earlier centuries, we have a wider extension together with a lower degree of intensity.

Another characteristic common to the countries under observation is that, whilst the graver crimes against property show a somewhat marked diminution, crimes against persons, on the other hand, show more steadiness, either of regularity, as in France and Belgium, or of increase, as in England, and still more in Germany. But this phenomenon in the case of crimes against the person is in actual correspondence with criminal activity arising from an increase of population. On the other hand-- apart from the transformation of crimes of violence into crimes of craft and fraud, due to the increase of movable property--the decrease of offences against property is no more than the manifest effect of an artificial change of judicial procedure, summary proceedings taking the place of trial by jury.

An alternation, which is not invalidated by exceptions here and there, has been observed in the criminality of different countries, in the periodic movement of crimes and offences against property and those against the person, of such a kind that years of increase in the former usually answer to a diminution in the latter, and vice versa. The principal factors in the annual increase of theft, such as scarcity and extremes of weather, cause a corresponding diminution of violent assaults and bodily harm, of homicides and indecent assaults, and vice versa. On the other hand, offences against property, which are very numerous, contribute most of all to the total of annual crime; so that the maximum of 1880 in Italy, as well as in France, Belgium and Austria, is especially due to the great severity of the winter of 1879-80, which in Italy coincided with an agricultural crisis, attested by the very high price of corn. Whereas from 1881 to 1885 there were very mild winters, with more abundant harvests, and from 1886 a greater extreme of cold and a more acute economic crisis.

The general tendency of these periodic oscillations of crime in Italy, as in other European countries, is nevertheless far more towards increase than towards decrease. This is also shown by the proportional triennial averages of crimes and offences placed on record, and of persons condemned to imprisonment.

In the movement of crime in each country it is necessary to distinguish special oscillations, more or less prolonged, of increase or decrease, from its general and permanent tendency. The latter is determined by the fundamental conditions of each nation, physical and social, apart from the purely artificial section of transgressions brought into existence by new laws. The special oscillations, on the other hand, are determined by the annual variations in this or that factor of the more numerous offences; that is to say, by abundance or scantiness of the harvests, by the annual variations of temperature, by industrial and political crises, and the like.

The oblivion of this marked distinction, coupled with the prejudices of the scientific schools, and even of political parties, leads to some curious disagreements, and to lively discussions on the results of criminal statistics. For on one side the champions of the classical school plainly see that the persistent increase of crimes and offences amounts to a proof of that breakdown of penal systems, practical and theoretical, which have hitherto been applied--as was admitted by Holtzendorff. And on the other hand, the increase of crimes is denied or affirmed for the purpose of supporting or attacking some particular ministry. For, in parliaments more than elsewhere, there is always a deep-seated and vivacious prejudice, a kind of social artificiality, which causes men to think that the condition of States, moral and economic, is fundamentally determined far more by the action of this or that government than by natural factors, which are mainly superior to and outside of governments and politicians.

And this is why in Italy there has been much discussion of late, in scientific publications, at the sittings of the Central Commission of Judicial Statistics, and even in Parliament, as to whether crime was increasing or decreasing.

Beltrani-Scalia and Lombroso almost simultaneously called attention to the growth of Italian crime, and they were succeeded by various adherents of the positive school, such as Ferri, Garofalo, Pavia, Pugliese, Guidi, Bournet, Barzilai, and Rossi, who produced evidence that the general tendency of crime in Italy was to increase, and that the diminutions observed after 1880 were mere transitory oscillations; and after 1886 they were justified by facts.

On the other hand, official returns of criminal statistics, and a majority of the members of the Central Commission, when pursuing an inquiry suggested by myself into Italian crime since 1873 --for previously to this date there are no criminal statistics in Italy except for 1853 and 1869-70--came to the conclusion that there was a tendency towards a diminution of crime. But their decision was formed from an entirely partial standpoint, which they had taken up in the exigency of polemical discussion. They compared, in fact, the years just concluded, 1881-5, with 1880, and thus it naturally followed that after a maximum they had a relative decrease. And it was only this ingenious comparison which gave an appearance of actual proof to their optimistic assertions; for when a fever is at forty degrees, the fall of even half a degree is very important. They paid special attention to the so-called high criminality, which is tried by the Assize courts, and is actually decreasing, though by the purely artificial effect of more and more effective measures of correction. But I have always maintained, and I have the support of M. Oettingen, that we cannot separate crimes and offences tried by the Assizes from those tried by the Tribunals, for there is only a difference of degree between them, as is clear in regard to theft, assaults and wounding, forgery and the like.

It is a curious fact that similar illusions have existed in all countries through the same causes and prejudices which have been mentioned above. In France, for instance, we often find that the keepers of the seals, reporting on volumes of the excellent and valuable series of criminal statistics since the year 1826, occasionally remark on these oscillatory diminutions, and make a point of treating them as signs of a constant and general tendency, which succeeding years have always contradicted.

In France also, the same controversy has been kept up since 1840, with the same polemical artifices as were employed more recently in Italy, on the question whether crime has increased or decreased. Dufau, Beranger, Berrzat de St. Prix, and Legoyt affirmed that it had diminished since 1826, against the true opinion of de Metz, Dupin, Chassan, Mesuard, and Fayet, the last of whom quotes the others in one of his essays on criminal statistics, now undeservedly forgotten, though they abound in striking and profound observation.

But, as for France in those days, so for Italy to-day, the statistics of succeeding years quickly proved that what official optimism and national self-complacency spoke of as pessimism on our part was but a conscientious inference from lamentable facts, established in every country by the influence of civilisation on crime, which I have described in preceding pages.

After these general statements we ought logically to watch the periodic movement of each leading category of crimes and offences in each division of the country; for not all crimes, nor all districts, pursue the same course from year to year. But as this inquiry is impossible in the present work, we may pass on to the general figures for other European countries.

FRAN 1826-8. 1895-7. Police Contraventions ... ... 100 391|
Offences ... ... 100 397| Crimes against the person ... ... 100 98|in 61 years

" property ... ... 100 41|

BELGIUM. 1850-2. 1883-5. Tried by the Correctional Tribunals,

for crimes against the person 100 109|in 36 years

" property ... 100 162|
1840-2. 1883-5.

Tried by the Tribunals for ``Offences'' 100 260| Tried at Assizes, crimes against the person 100 65|in 46 years " " property 100 21|

ENGLAND. 1857-9. 1884-6. Tried summarily, for offences ... 100 176 in 30 years.

1835-7. 1884-6.

Criminal cases, against the person 100 143| " against property, and for |in 55 years. circulation of false money ... 100 55|

IRELAND. 1864-6. 1886-8. Tried summarily ... ... 100 95| Crimes against the person ... .. 100 57|in 25 years.

" property, and false money 100 52|

PRUSSIA. 1854-6. 1876-8. Contraventions and ``vols de bois'' 100 132|in 25 years. Crimes and offences ... ... 100 134|

GERMANY. 1882-4. 1885-7. Crimes and offences against public order 100 110|

" " the person 100 116|in 6 years.
" " property 100 95|

AUSTRIA. 1867-9. 1884-6. Prisoners condemned for crimes -- 100 122|in 20 years.

" " offences ... 100 495|

SPAIN. 1883-4. 1886-7. Tried for crimes and offences -- 100 {X}3|in 5 years.

" contraventions ...... 100 113|

The most constant general fact shown by these data is in all cases the very remarkable increase of slighter delinquencies, side by side with constancy or slight diminution in crimes against the person, and a large diminution in crime against property. This is seen in France, England, Belgium, whilst there is an increase both of crimes and offences in Austria.

41

Behind the general fact, however, we must distinguish between the actual and the apparent.

On the one hand, the decrease of more serious crime against property is simply due to prisoners electing to be sentenced by the inferior court, which is at the discretion of the Tribunals in France, but legally established in Belgium, by the laws of 1838 and 1848, and in England by the Acts of 1856 and 1878--an election of the slighter but more certain punishment of the magistrates in preference to going before a jury. Indeed, crimes against the person, in which there is less power of election, do not exhibit so marked a decrease; and accordingly we see that in Belgium the increase of ``correctionalised" crimes is due far more to crimes against property (62 per cent in 36 years) than to those against the person (9 per cent.).

On the other hand, the growth of slighter delinquency is partly the effect of special enactments, which are constantly creating new infractions, offences or contraventions. For France may be mentioned the law of 1832 on eluding supervision, that of 1844 on the game laws, that of 1857 on the false description of goods for sale, of 1845 on railway offences, of 1849 on the expulsion of refugees, of 1873 on drunkenness, and of 1874 on requisition of horses. I dealt with the statistical results of these laws, and with the influence of the increasing number of police agents, in my ``Studies on Criminality in France" (Rome, 1881); and I will here add only a single observation. If it is true, as M. Joly says, that other laws, passed since 1826, have extinguished a few offences, or at least have diminished their frequency under less severe regulations, yet it is also true that the new infractions created in the past half-century show far higher numbers than those of the infractions which have been extinguished or rendered less easy. So that amongst the 297 per cent. of increase on the offences tried in France between 1826 and 1887, the element due to legal creation of new infractions must not be ignored.

It cannot, however, be denied that for certain more frequent offences we have a real and very noteworthy increase, apart from any legislative or statistical cause of disturbance.

The same observation may be made in regard to England. There also the increase of 76 per cent, during thirty years of offences tried summarily is due in part to new infractions, created by special legislation, and especially by the Education Act of 1873, under which there were more than forty thousand infractions in 1878, and more than sixty-five thousand in 1886.

In regard to this delinquency in England (wherein are included, over and above real offences, certain infractions corresponding to the police contraventions of the Italian, French, Belgian and Austrian codes) it is to be observed that the increase of 76 per cent. in thirty years is due rather to contraventions than to offences. And this

42

would establish a remarkable difference between the variations of delinquency in England and in France.

If we analyse the record of infractions tried summarily in England, we find that contraventions of the law in respect of drunkenness account for most of this increase (from 82,196 in 1861 to 183,221 in 1885 and 165,139 in 1886). On the other hand, offences against the person (assaults) and against property (stealing, larceny, malicious offences) have not shown so large an increase.

In fact, if we compare the variations in assaults and thefts in France and England, we have the following figures:--

ENGLAND.

1861-3. 1879-81.

Prisoners tried summarily for assaults ... ... 100 102 Ditto for stealing, larceny, and malicious

offences 100 110

FRANCE. Cases tried by the Tribunals: For assault and wounding ... ... 100 134 For simple theft 100 116

So that in England not only the total delinquency, but more especially the commoner offences against the person and against property show a slighter increase than that which has been established for the same period in France. Whilst we do not overlook the greater increase of crimes against the person in England (coinciding, of course, with the doubling of the population in fifty-five years), this fact seems to me to prove the salutary influence of English organisations against certain social factors which lead up to delinquency (such as the care of foundlings, the guardianship of the poor, and so forth), notwithstanding the great development of economic activity, which is assuredly in no way inferior to that of France. The figures strengthen my conclusions as to the social factors of crime, and refute the optimistic theory of Poletti.

But the actual participation of each country in the general increase of crime in Europe is determined by other causes, outside of the artificial influences of different codes of law. And the most general and constant of these causes, in all the various physical and social environments, is the annual increase of population, which, by adding to the density of the inhabitants of each country, multiplies their material and legal relations to one another, and, consequently, the objective and subjective constituents of crime.

Taking the official Italian figures, which are also relied on by M. Levasseur, we find, for the periods corresponding to the variations of criminality, the following rates of increase in the population of the different countries. Ireland shows a decrease, owing to emigration.

Increase.

Italy 22,104,789 in 1863--30,947,306 in 1889 40 per cent. " 27,165,553 in 1873--30,565,188 in 1888 12 " France 31,858,937 in 1826--38,218,903 in 1887 20 per cent. Belgium 4,072,619 in 1840-- 5,583,278 in 1885 44 " Prussia 21,046,984 in 1852--26,614,428 in 1878 26 " Germany 45,717,000 in 1882--47,540,000 in 1887 4 " England 13,896,797 in 1831--27,870,586 in 1886 101 " " 20,066,224 in 1861--27,870,586 in 1886 39 " Austria 20,217,531 in 1869--23,070,688 in 1886 14 " Ireland 5,798,967 in 1861-- 4,777,545 in 1888 decrease 17 "

It must, however, be observed, with regard to this increase of the population, firstly that it tells as a factor of criminality only in so far as it is not neutralised, wholly or in part, by other influences, mainly social, which prevent crime or render it less grave. Secondly, it is not right merely to compare the proportional rates of increase in the population with those of crime, as was done for instance by M. Bodio, who said that in Italy, from 1873 to 1883, ``since the population had increased by 7.5 per cent., crime might have increased during the same time by 7.5 per cent., without its being fair to say that it had actually increased." In point of fact, as M. Rossi remarked, since in Italy, and almost all the European States, the growth of the population is due to the excess of births over deaths (for emigration is more numerous than immigration), it is evident that, when we confine our attention to short periods, the addition to the population, consisting of children under ten or twelve years, does not increase crime in an appreciable degree. The deaths, on the other hand, must be subtracted from all stages of human life, but especially from the number of those who can and do commit crimes and offences.

Now, as we cannot in this place go into detail, I must confine myself to the statement of a few characteristic facts, as illustrated by European crime. Thus we perceive the influence of the great famine of 1846-7 on crimes against property in France and Belgium; the rapid oscillations of crime in Ireland, indicating the unstable political and social conditions of the country; and the parallel movements of crime in, France and Prussia. We see, indeed, a constant diminution of crime for the period between 1860 and 1870, followed (after the statistical disturbance of the terrible year 1870-1) by a period of serious and continued increase of crime, resulting from social and economic conditions, as shown especially by the increase of vagrancy and theft since 1875.

All these general facts go to prove the close and intimate connection between crime and the aggregate of its various constituents. So that, without pursuing more detailed inquiries into certain social factors of crime, which are capable of statistical enumeration, such as the increase in the number of the police, the abundance or scarcity of corn and wine, the spread of drunkenness, family circumstances, increase of personal possessions, the facility or otherwise of the settlement of disputes, commercial and industrial crises, the rate of wages, the variation from year to year of the general conditions of existence, and so forth, coincident with the development of education, encouragements to thrift and the organisation of charity, we must now proceed to draw from these statistical data the most important conclusions of criminal sociology.

I.

Criminal statistics show that crime increases in the aggregate, with more or less notable oscillations from year to year, rising or falling in successive waves. Thus it is evident that the level of criminality in any one year is determined by the different conditions of the physical and social environment, combined with the hereditary tendencies and occasional impulses of the individual, in obedience to a law which I have called, in analogy with chemical phenomena, the law of criminal saturation.

Just as in a given volume of water, at a given temperature, we find a solution of a fixed quantity of any chemical substance, not an atom more or less, so in a given social environment, in certain defined physical conditions of the individual, we find the commission of a fixed number of crimes.

Our ignorance of many physical and psychical laws and of innumerable conditions of fact, will prevent us from obtaining a precise view of this level of criminality. But none the less is it the necessary and inevitable result of a given physical and social environment. Statistics show us, indeed, that the variations of this environment are always attended by consequential and proportional variations of crime. In France, for instance (and the observation will be found to apply to every country which possesses an extended series of criminal statistics), the number of crimes against the person varies but little in sixty-two years. The same thing holds good for England and Belgium, because their special environment is also less variable, by reason that hereditary dispositions and human passions cannot vary profoundly or frequently, except under the influence of exceptional disturbances of the weather, or of social conditions. In fact, the more serious variations in respect of crimes against the person in France have taken place either during political revolutions, or in years of excessive heat, or of exceptional abundance of meat, grain, and wine. This is illustrated by the exceptional increase of crime from 1849 to 1852. Minor offences against the person, on the contrary, which are more occasional, assaults and wounding, for example, vary in the main, as to their annual oscillations, with the abundance of the wine harvest, whilst in their oscillations from month to month they display a characteristic increase during the vintage periods, from June

45

to December, notwithstanding the constant diminution of other offences and crimes against the person.

On the other hand, crimes against property, and still more offences against property, show wide oscillations on account of the variability of the special environment, which is almost always in a condition of unstable equilibrium, as in periods of scarcity, and of commercial, financial and industrial crises, and so forth, whilst they are subject also to the influence of the physical environment. Crimes and offences against property display extraordinary increases in the severest winter seasons, and diminutions in milder winters.

And this correspondence between the more general, powerful, and variable physical and social factors of crime, as well as its more characteristic manifestations such as thefts, wounding, and indecent assaults, is so constant and so direct that, when I was studying the annual movement of criminality in France, and perceived some extraordinary oscillation in the crimes and offences, I foresaw that in the annals of the year I should find mention of an agricultural or political crisis, or an exceptional winter or summer in the records of the weather. So that with a single column of a table of criminal statistics I was able to reconstruct the historical condition of a country in its more salient features. In this way psychological experiment again confirmed the truth of the law of criminal saturation.

Not only so, but it may be added that as, in chemistry, over and above the normal saturation we find that an increased temperature of the liquid envelopes an exceptional super-saturation, so in criminal sociology, in addition to the ordinary saturation we are sometimes aware of an excess of criminal saturation, due to the exceptional conditions of the social environment.

Indeed it is to be observed not only that the main and typical criminality has a sort of reflex criminality depending upon it, but also that an increase of more serious or more frequent crimes induces a crop of resistance to and assaults upon the guardians of public order, together with false witness, insults, avoidance of supervision, absconding, and the like. Certain crimes and offences also have their complementary offences, which from being consequences become in their turn the causes of new offences. Thus concealment and purchase of stolen goods increase simultaneously with theft; homicide and wounding lead to the illegal carrying of arms; adultery and abusive language to duels, and so forth.

Beyond this there are sundry kinds of excessive criminal saturations which are exceptional, and therefore transitory. Ireland and Russia present us with conspicuous examples in their political and social crimes; and similarly America, during election contests. So in France before and after December 2 1851, the harbouring of criminals, which in no other quadrennial period from 1826 to 1887 exceeds a record of fifty, rises in 1850-53 as high as 239. So during the famine of 1847, theft of

46

grain rises in France to forty-two in a single year, whilst for half a century it barely reaches a total of seventy-five. It is notorious, again, that in years of dear provisions, or severe winters, a large number of thefts and petty offences are committed for the sole object of securing maintenance within the prison walls. And in this connection I have observed in France that other offences against property decrease during a famine, by an analogous psychological motive, thus presenting a sort of statistical paradox. Thus, for example, I have found that as oidium and phylloxera are more effective than severe punishments in diminishing the number of assaults and cases of unlawful wounding, so famine succeeds better than the strongest bars, or dogs kept loose in the prison yards, in preventing the escape of prisoners, who at such times are detained by the advantage of being supported at the public expense.

For a parallel reason in 1847, a famine year, whilst all crimes and offences against property increased in an extraordinary fashion, only the crimes of theft and breach of confidence by household servants showed a characteristic decrease, because such persons were deterred by the fear of being dismissed by their employers during the time of distress. The figures are as follows:--

FRANCE (Assizes). 1844. 1845. 1846. 1847. Crimes against property ... 3,767 3,396 3,581 4,235 Breach of confidence by household servants ... ... 136 128 168 104 Thefts by the same 1,001 874 924 896

M. Chaussinand adds, by way of confirmation of my statement that during economic crises, such as famine and high prices of grain, the number of cases of escape from justice also decreases, FOR ``thieves and tramps prefer arrest, in order to escape from the misery which afflicts them outside the prison walls."

Two fundamental conclusions of criminal sociology may be drawn from this law of criminal saturation.

The first is that it is incorrect to assert a mechanical regularity of crime, which from Quetelet's time has been much exaggerated. There has been a too literal insistance on his famous declaration that ``the budget of crime is an annual taxation paid with more preciseness than any other"; and that it is possible to calculate beforehand how many homicides, poisoners, and forgers we shall have, because ``crimes are generated every year in the same number, with the same punishments, in the same proportions." And one constantly meets with this echo of the statisticians, that ``from year to year crimes against the person vary at the most by one in twenty-five, and those against property by one in fifty"; or, again, that there is ``a law of limitation in crime, which does not vary by more than one in ten."

This opinion, originated by Quetelet and other statisticians after an inquiry confined to the more serious crimes, and to a very short succession of years, has already been refuted, in part by Maury and Rhenisch, and more plainly by Aberdare, Mayr, Messedaglia and Minzloff.

In fact, if the level of criminality is of necessity determined by the physical and social environment, how could it remain constant in spite of the continual variations, sometimes very considerable, of this same environment? That which does remain fixed is the proportion between a given environment and the number of crimes: and this is precisely the law of criminal saturation. But the statistics of criminality will never be constant to one rule from year to year. There will be a dynamical but not a statical regularity.

Thus the element of fixity in criminal sociology consists in asserting, not the fatality or predestination of human actions, including crimes, but only their necessary dependence upon their natural causes, and therewith the possibility of modifying effects by modifying the activity of these causes. And, indeed, even Quetelet himself recognised this when he said, ``If we change the social order we shall see an immediate change in the facts which have been so constantly reproduced. Statisticians will then have to consider whether the changes have been useful or injurious. These studies therefore show how important is the mission of the legislator, and how responsible he is in his own sphere for all the phenomena of the social order.''

The second consequence of the law of criminal saturation, one of great theoretical importance, is that the penalties hitherto regarded, save for a few platonic declarations, as the best remedies for crime, are less effectual than they are supposed to be. For crimes and offences increase and diminish by a combination of other causes, which are far from being identical with the punishments lightly written out by legislators and awarded by judges.

History affords us various impressive examples.

The Roman Empire, when society had fallen into extreme corruption, recalling many symptoms of our own epoch, vainly promulgated laws which visited celibacy, adultery, and incest--``venus prodigiosa''--with ``the vengeance of the sword and punishments of the utmost severity.'' Dio Cassius (``Hist. Rom.,'' lxxvi. 16) says that in the city of Rome alone, after the law of Septimus Severus, there were three thousand charges of adultery. But the stringent laws against these crimes continued to the days of Justinian, which shows that the crimes had not been checked; and, as Gibbon says (``Decline and Fall,'' ch. 44), the Scatinian law against ``venus nefanda'' had fallen into abeyance through lapse of time and the multitude of offenders. Yet we see in our own days, as in France, that there are some who would oppose celibacy with no other remedy than a law passed for the purpose.

Since mediaeval times the increasing gentleness of manners has caused a diminution of crimes of blood, once so numerous that there was need of sundry ``truces'' and ``peaces,'' notwithstanding the harsh penalties of previous centuries. And Du Boys called Cettes simple because, after giving a table of shocking punishments in the Germany of his day (the fifteenth century), he marvelled that all these pains and torments had not prevented the increase of crimes.

Imperial Rome deluded herself with the idea that she could stamp out Christianity with punishments and tortures, which, however, only seemed to fan the flame. In the same way Catholic Europe hoped to extinguish Protestantism by means of vindictive persecution, and only produced the opposite effect, as always happens. If the Reformed faith does not strike root in Italy, France, and Spain, that must be explained by psychological reasons proper to those nations, independently of the stake and of massacres, for it did not strike root even when religious belief was liberated from its fetters. This does not prevent all governments in every land from continuing to believe that, in order to arrest the spread of certain political or social doctrines, there is nothing better than to pass exceptional penal laws, forgetting that, with ideas and prejudices just as with steam, compression increases the expansive force.

Popular education has swept away the so-called crimes of magic and witchcraft, though they had withstood the most savage punishments of antiquity and mediaeval times.

Blasphemy, in spite of the slitting of the nose, tongue, and lips, enacted by the penal laws, and continued in France from Louis XI. to Louis XV., was very common in the middle ages, being (like witchcraft, trances, and self-immurement) a pathological or abnormal manifestation of religious emotion, which in those times had an extraordinary development. And the habit of blasphemy diminished under the psychological and social evolution of our own days, precisely when it ceased to be punished. Or, rather, it continued to this day, as in Tuscany, where the Tuscan penal code (Art. 136), which survived until December 31, 1889, still punished it with five years' imprisonment. The illusion as to the efficacy of punishment is so deeply rooted that a proposal was made in the Senate, in 1875, to include this penalty in the new Italian penal code. And at Murcia, in Spain, trials for blasphemy have lately been re-established.

Mittermaier observed that, if in England and Scotland there were far fewer cases of false witness, perjury, and resistance to authority than in Ireland and on the Continent, this must be due in great measure to national character, which is one of the hereditary elements of normal as well as of abnormal and criminal life.

Thus even apart from statistics we can satisfy ourselves that crimes and punishments belong to two different spheres; but when statistics support the teaching of history, no doubt can remain as to the very slight (I had almost said the absence of any) deterrent effect of punishments upon crime.

We may indeed derive a telling proof from statistical records, by referring to the progress of repression in France, over a period of sixty years, as I have already done in my ``Studies'' previously quoted.

When we speak of the repression of crime, we must first of all distinguish between that which is due to the general character of penal legislation, more or less severe, and that which is secured by the administration by the judges of the law as it is. Now, so far as legislation is concerned, the growth of crime in France certainly cannot be attributed to the relaxation of punishment. The legislative reforms which have taken place, especially in 1832 and 1863, on the general revision of the penal code, modified punishments to some extent, but with the definite purpose and result, as shown by the same official records of criminal statistics, of strengthening the repressive power of the law by providing for the application of less aggravated punishments. The repugnance of juries and judges against excessive punishments, and their preference for acquittal, is, indeed, a psychological law. Moreover, it is well known that if there is in Europe a penal code less mild than any of the rest, it is that of France, which is the oldest of those now in force, and still retains much of the military rigour of its origin. And it must be added that for certain crimes, as for rapes and indecent assaults, which are nevertheless constantly increasing in France, the punishments have been increased by several successive enactments. The same is true of extortion by threats of exposure, which occurs more and more frequently, as M. Joly also observes, in spite of the severe punishments of the law of 1863.

The question, therefore, is reduced to judicial repression, the progress whereof must be observed in the past half-century, for it has evidently the greatest influence upon crime. Laws, in fact, have no real operation if they are not applied more or less rigorously; for in the social strata which contribute most to criminality the laws are known only by their practical application, which is also the only truly defensive function, carrying with it a special preventive of the repetition of the crime by the person condemned.

Thus the arguments of jurists and legislators have not much value for the criminal sociologist when they are based solely on the psychological illusion that the dangerous classes trouble themselves about the shaping of a penal code, as the more instructed and less numerous classes might well do. The dangerous classes attend to the sentences of the judges, and still more to the execution of those sentences, than to the articles of a code. In this connection I cannot agree with the forecast of Garofalo as to the perilous effect of the abolition of capital punishment in Italy on the imagination of the people; for he was well aware that, though it is defined in various articles of the old code, and in about sixty sentences every year, the punishment of death has not been carried out, which is the essential point, for the last fifteen years.

The elements which determine the greater or less severity of judicial repression are of two kinds:--

1. The ratio of persons acquitted to the total number of prisoners put on their trial.

2. The ratio of the severest punishments to the total number of prisoners condemned.

Certainly the proportion of acquittals ought not to indicate a difference in the severity of repression as such, for condemnation or acquittal ought to point merely to the certainty or otherwise of guilt, the sufficiency or insufficiency of the evidence. But, as a matter of fact, the proportional increase of convictions does partly represent greater severity on the part of the judges, and still more of the juries, who display it by attaching weight to somewhat unconvincing evidence, or in too readily admitting circumstances which tend to aggravate the offence. This is confirmed also by the rarity of acquittals in cases of contumacy.

Of these two factors the former is certainly the more important, for it is a psychological law that man, in regard to punishment as to any other kind of suffering, is more affected by the certainty than by the gravity of the infliction. And it is to the credit of criminal theorists of the classical school that they have steadily maintained that a mild yet certain punishment is more effectual than one which, being severe in itself, holds out a stronger hope of escaping it. Nevertheless it is a fact that they have carried the theory too far, by seeking to obtain excessive mitigations and abbreviations of punishment, without exerting themselves to secure certainty by reforms of procedure and police administration.

The diminution of the rate of acquittal is evident and continuous, both at the Assizes and in the Tribunals, except for the last quadrennial period. This may of course indicate a more careful management of the trials by the judges; but it certainly shows an undoubted tendency towards increased judicial severity, which, meanwhile, has not arrested the growth of crime.

PERCENTAGE OF ACQUITTALS IN FRANCE.

Tried in		
Assize Courts.	Tribunals.	Total
1826-30 39	 31	 32
1831-5 42	 28	 30
1836-40 35	 22	 23
1841-5 32	 18	 19
1846-50 36	 16	 17

1851-5 ... ... 28 ... ... 12 13
1856-60 ... ... 24 ... ... 10 7
1861-5 ... ... 24 ... ... 9 6
1866-9 ... ... 23 ... ... 17 8
1872-6 ... ... 20 ... ... 6 6
1877-81 ... ... 23 ... ... 5 6
1882-6 ... ... 27 ... ... 6 6

PERCENTAGE OF ACQUITTALS IN ENGLAND.

Criminal Proceedings. Summary Proceedings.
1858-62 ... ... 25 34
1863-7 ... ... 24 31
1868-72 ... ... 26 24
1873-7 ... ... 25 21
1878-82 ... ... 24 21
1883-7 ... ... 22 20

Here also it appears that the growth of crime in England, though less than in France, is not due to the weakening of judicial severity through the greater number of acquittals. The number has, in fact, constantly diminished, especially in summary proceedings, which is just where the greatest increase of crime is manifest.

Passing now to the other factor of judicial repression, that is to the percentage of persons sentenced to graver kinds of punishment, we have to take into account, amongst assize cases in France, the prisoners sentenced to death, penal servitude, and solitary imprisonment, excluding such as are sentenced to correctional punishment (simple imprisonment and fines) as well as young prisoners sent to reformatories; and in regard to the Tribunals, we must take the percentages of those who are condemned to imprisonment, which is the most serious punishment, the remainder being fined, or handed over to their parents, or sent to reformatories.

Condemned at Assizes Condemned

FRANCE. --------------------------- by Tribunals

To death. To penal servitude. to imprisonment.

1826-30 ... ... 2.5 ... ... 58 61

1831-5 ... ... 1.5 ... ... 42 65

1836-40 ... ... .7 ... ... 37 65

1841-5 ... ... 1 ... ... 40 61

1845-50 ... ... 1 ... ... 39 62

1851-5 ... ... 1.1 ... ... 48 61

1856-60 ... ... 1 ... ... 49 61

1861-5 ... ... .6 ... ... 48 64

1866-9 ... ... .5 ... ... 47 68

1872-6 ... ... .7 ... ... 49 66

1877-81 ... ... .7 ... ... 50 66

1882-6 ... ... 1 ... ... 49 65

These figures, if they do not show (as might have been foreseen) so large an increase of severity as in the percentages of acquittals, yet prove that repression has not diminished even in the serious character of the punishments. On the other hand, we can see that, in the assize cases, excluding the first period, before the revision of 1832, whilst capital punishment shows a certain diminution (especially due to the laws of 1832, 1848, &c., which reduced the number of cases involving the death penalty), though continuing at a certain level since 1861, sentences of penal servitude and solitary confinement show a continued increase from the second period, and especially since 1851.

So also at the Tribunals, except for a few oscillations, as in the ninth period, there is a sustained increase of repression.

And the fact that this increased ratio of the more serious punishments actually indicates a greater severity on the part of the judges can only be contested on the ground of a simultaneous increase of the more serious crimes and offences. On the other hand, we note in France a general decrease of crimes against the person (except for assaults on children), and still more of crimes against property.

There is also a striking confirmation in the corresponding acquittals and condemnations of a more serious character. We see, in fact, that the more serious condemnations increase precisely when the acquittals decrease (as in the 4th, 6th, 7th, and 10th periods at the Assizes, and the 2nd, 5th, and 8th periods at the

53

Tribunals); whilst in the years of more frequent acquittals there is also a diminution of more serious punishments, as in the 5th and 8th periods at the Assizes. That is to say, the two sets of statistics actually indicate a greater or less severity on the part of juries and judges.

This firmer repression is demonstrated in spite of the continued increase of attenuating circumstances, which rose at the Assizes from 50 per cent. in 1833 to 73 per cent. in 1806, and at the Tribunals from 54 per cent. in 1851 to 65 per cent. in 1886. Nevertheless it is a fact that the number of cases tried by default at the Assizes has continuously decreased from a yearly average of 647 in 1826-30 to one of 266 in 1882-6.

For Italy we have the following figures: {column missing head?}

PRETORS. TRIBUNALS. ASSIZES.

Condemned to Imprisonment. Condemned Penal Servitude

Slighter imprisonment. to death. for life. temporary punishts 1874 21 79 1.2 5.6 65 28 5 22 80 1.3 6.5 63 29 6 23 81 1.3 6.1 66 27 7 24 82 1.5 7.2 66 25 8 25 85 1 7.6 67 25 9 25 -- 1.2 6.3 67 25 1880 26 -- 1.3 5.5 68 25 1 24 81 1.7 6.1 65 27 2 23 81 1.5 6 66 27 3 23 81 1.7 5.4 64 29 4 23 81 1.3 5.3 64 30 5 23 81 1.6 5.4 63 30 6 21 81 1.6 5.7 62 30 7 21 83 1.1 5.8 63 30 8 21 82 1.2 4.7 65 29

Thus, once more, there has been no relaxation of repression, except in late years for those condemned by the Pretors to penal servitude for life.

The conclusion, therefore, is still the same, namely that judicial repression, in France and Italy, has grown stronger and stronger, whilst criminality has increased more and more.

In this fact, again, which confutes the common opinion that the sovereign remedy of crime is the greater rigour of punishment, we may fairly find a positive proof that the penal, legislative, and administrative systems hitherto adopted have missed their aim, which can be nothing else than the defence of society against criminals.

Henceforth we must seek, through the study of facts, a better direction for penal legislation as a function of society, so that, by the observation of psychological and sociological laws, it may tend, not to a violent and always tardy reaction against crime already evolved, but to the elimination or diversion of its natural factors.

This fundamental conclusion of criminal statistics is so important that we must confirm it by adding to the statistical data the general laws of biology and sociology.

This is the more necessary because my position as first stated has met with some criticism.

In the first place, it is easily seen, when we compare the total result of crime with the varied character of its anthropological, physical, and social factors, that punishment can exert but a slight influence upon it. Punishment, in fact, by its special effect as a legal deterrent, acting as a psychological motive, will clearly be unable to neutralise the constant and hereditary action of climate, customs, increase of population, agricultural production, economic and political crises, which statistics invariably exhibit as the most potent factors of the growth or diminution of criminality.

It is a natural law that forces cannot conflict or neutralise each other unless they are of the same kind. The fall of a body cannot be retarded, changed in direction or accelerated, save by a force homogeneous with that of gravity. So punishment, as a psychological motive, can only oppose the psychological factors of crime, and indeed only the occasional and moderately energetic factors; for it is evident that it cannot, as a preliminary to its application, eliminate the organic hereditary factors which are revealed to us by criminal anthropology.

Punishment, which has professed to be such a simple and powerful remedy against all the factors of crime, is therefore a panacea whose potency is far beneath its reputation.

We must bear in mind a fact which is familiar enough, though it has been too often forgotten by legislators and criminalists. Society is not a homogeneous aggregate, but on the contrary an organism, like every animal organism, composed of tissues of varying structure and sensibility. Every society, in fact, with its progressive and increasingly distinctive needs and occupations, is a product of the union of social classes which differ greatly in their organic and psychical characteristics. The physical constitution, the habits, sentiments, ideas, and tendencies of one social stratum are far from being the same as those of other strata. Here again we have, as Spencer would say, the law of evolution through a departure from the homogeneous to the heterogeneous, from the simple to the complex, or, in the words of Ardigo, a natural formation by successive distinctions. Amongst savage tribes this distinction of the social strata does not exist, or it is far less marked than in barbarian societies, and still less than in civilised societies.

Every schoolmaster with a bent for psychological observation separates his pupils into three classes. There is the class of industrious pupils of good disposition, who work of their own accord, without calling for strict discipline; that of the ignorant and idle (degenerate and of weak nervous force) from whom neither mildness nor severity can obtain anything worth having; and that of the pupils who are neither wholly industrious nor wholly idle, and for whom a discipline based on psychological laws may be genuinely useful.

This is the case with large bodies of soldiers or of prisoners, for all associations of men, and for society as a whole. These partial organisms, due to the constant relationships of a life more or less in common, are in this respect reproductions of society as a whole, just as a fragment of crystal reproduces the characteristics of the unbroken crystal.[13]

[13] There is, however, some difference between the manifestation of the activity of a group of men and that of the aggregate society. Between psychology which studies the individual, and sociology which studies the society, I think there is room for a collective psychology, to study more or less defined groups. The phenomena of these groups are analogous, but not identical with those of the sociological body properly so called, according as the union is more or less definite. Collective psychology has its field of observation in all unions, however occasional, such as the public street, the markets, workshops, theatres meetings, assemblies, colleges, schools, barracks, prisons, and so forth. Many practical applications of the data of collective psychology might be given. An example will be found in a future chapter, when I come to consider the psychology of the jury.

In the same way, from the standpoint of criminal sociology, we may divide the social strata into three analogous categories--the highest, which commits no crimes, organically upright, restrained only by the authority of the moral sense, of religious sentiments and public opinion, together with the hereditary transmission of moral habits. This class, for which no penal code would be necessary, is unfortunately very small; and it is far smaller if, in addition to legal and apparent criminality, we also take into account that social and latent criminality through which many men, who are upright so far as the penal code is concerned, are not upright by the standard of morality.

Another class, the lowest, is made up of individuals opposed to all sense of uprightness, who, being without education, perpetually dragged back by their material and moral destitution into the primitive forms of the brute struggle for existence, inherit from their parents and transmit to their children an abnormal organisation, adding degeneration and disease, an atavistic return to savage humanity. This is the nursery of the born criminals, for whom punishments, so far as they are legal deterrents, are useless, because they encounter no moral sense which could distinguish punishment by law from the risk which also attends upon every honest industry.

Lastly we have the other class of individuals who are not born to crime, but are not firmly upright, alternating between vice and virtue, with imperfect moral sense, education and training, for whom punishment may be genuinely useful as a psychological motive. It is just this class which yields the large contingent of occasional criminals, for whom punishments are efficacious if they are directed in their execution by the axioms of scientific psychology, and especially if they are aided by the social prevention which reduces the number of opportunities of committing crimes and offences.

Once again I must express my agreement with M. Garofalo, who, in dealing with this subject, insists on the necessity of distinguishing between the different classes of criminals before deciding as to the efficacy of punishments.

Yet this conclusion as to the very limited efficiency of punishments, which is forced upon us by facts, and which, as Bentham said, is confirmed by the application of each punitive act, precisely because its previous application did not succeed in preventing crime, is directly opposed to general public opinion, and even to the opinion of jurists and legislators.

On the inception or the growth of a criminal manifestation, legislators, jurists, and public think only of the remedies, which are as easy as they are illusory, of the penal code, or of some new Act of repression. Even if this were useful, which is very problematical, it has the inevitable disadvantage of making men ignore other remedies, far more profitable, albeit more difficult, of a preventive and social kind. And this tendency is so common that many of those who have dwelt upon or accepted the positive movement of the new school, not long after they had admitted that I was in the right, declared impulsively that ``the constant commission of crime arises from the lack of timely repression," and that ``one of the chief causes of the growth of crime in Italy is the mildness of our punishments." Or else they forgot to ask themselves the elementary question of criminal sociology, whether and how far punishments have a genuinely defensive force. This is just what happens with pedagogues who enter upon long discussions on the various methods and means of education, without asking themselves beforehand whether and how far education has the actual power of modifying the temperament and character which heredity stamps upon every individual.

These conclusions take us far beyond the limit of penal severity, and at the same time they suffice to combat the objection commonly raised against those who think, like ourselves, that repressive justice ought to concern itself not with the punishment of past crime, but with the prevention of future crime. For whilst the advocates of severity, and those whom I will call the ``laxativists," virtually think (apart from a few platonic statements) only of punishments as remedies of offences, we on the other hand believe that punishments are merely secondary instruments of social self-defence, and remedies ought to be adapted to the actual factors of the offence. And since the social factors are most capable of modification, so we say with Prins that ``for social evils we require social cures."

M. Tarde, then, was not quite accurate in his remark that my conviction as to the very slight efficacy of punishments is a mere consequence of my ideas on the anthropological and physical character of crime, and that, ``on the contrary, the preponderating importance which he has assigned to the social causes logically debars him from accepting this conclusion." As a matter of fact, punishment regarded as a psychological motive so far as it is a legal deterrent, and as a physical motive so far as it implies the confinement of the person condemned, would more naturally belong, in abstract logic, to the biological and physical theory of crime. Whereas it is precisely because I recognise the influence of social environment, in addition, that experimental logic convinces me that punishment is not an efficacious remedy of crime, unless forces are applied beforehand to neutralise, or at any rate to counteract, the social factors of crime.

And if this is not a new conclusion, as one of our critics observes by way of reproach--as though it were not one of the characteristics of truth to repeat itself persistently, however much it may be forgotten or even opposed--we must nevertheless remark that it is now repeated with a mass of new observations and definite applications, which give it a force unknown to mere logical deductions.

The classical school has concerned itself simply with mitigation of punishment as compared with mediaeval excess; and for this reason, because every age has its own mission, it could not also concern itself with the prevention of crimes, which is far more useful and efficacious. A few isolated thinkers, it is true, wrote a few bold and far-reaching pages on preventive methods in opposition to the numerous volumes on punishment; but their words had no effect upon criminalists and legislators, because science had not yet undertaken the positive and methodical observation of the natural factors of crime.

I will confine myself to a few examples, in order to show that amongst practical men, as amongst public officials and legislators, the illusion that punishments are the true panacea of crime is always predominant.

Practical men declare that ``the prohibitive penal law ought to be regarded as the first and most important of preventive laws." The prefets in their circulars, being concerned about the increase of crime, put forward the most vigilant and severe repression as a sovereign remedy. A counsellor of the French Cour de Cassation writes that ``in a worthy system of social police there is no better guarantee for order and safety than intimidation." The Keeper of the Seals, in his report on French penal statistics for 1876, speaking of the continued increase of indecent assaults, comes to the conclusion that ``in any case, only firm and energetic repression can avail against a lamentable increase of crimes against morality." And more recently another Keeper of the Seals ended his report on the statistics of 1826 to 1880 by observing that ``the growth of crime can only be opposed by an incessantly vigorous repression." M. Tarde agreed with this conclusion, saying that ``if crimes are only, as has been said, railway accidents of a society travelling at full speed, it must not be forgotten that, the faster the train, the stronger must be the brake . . . and it is certain that such a state of affairs demands an increase or a new departure of repression and punishment."

It may be admitted that our conclusion is not a novelty; but, as Stuart Mill said, there are two ways of effecting useful innovations, to discover what was not known before, or else to repeat with new demonstrations the truths which had been forgotten.

And this illusion as to the influence of punishments is so widespread that it is well to inquire into its historic and psychological arguments; for, as Spencer says, in order to decide as to the value of an idea, it is useful to examine its genealogy.

We may pass by the foundation of primitive vengeance, which from the age of private combats passed into the spirit and form of the earliest penal laws, and still subsists as a more or less unconscious and enfeebled residuum in modern society. We may also pass by the hereditary effect of the traditions of mediaeval severity, which excite an instinctive sympathy for stern punishment in connection with every crime.

But one of the main reasons of this tendency is an error of psychological perspective, whereby men have forgotten the profound differences of the ideas, habits, and sentiments of the various social strata, concerning which I have spoken above. Through this forgetfulness the honest and instructed classes confound their own idea of the penal law, and the impression it makes upon them, with the idea and the impression of the social classes from which the majority of criminals are recruited. This has been remarked upon by Beccaria, Carmignani, and Holtzendorff amongst the classical criminalists, and by Lombroso and others of the new school who have studied the slang and literature of criminals, which are their psychological mirror. Again, it is forgotten that for the higher classes, apart from their physical and moral repugnance against crime, which is the most powerful repelling force, there is the fear of public opinion, almost unknown amongst the classes which have stopped short at a lower stage of human evolution.

For the higher classes one example may suffice. It is the fact observed upon by Mr. Spencer, that gambling debts and Stock Exchange bargains are scrupulously discharged, though for them there is neither penal obligation nor evidence in writing. And it may be added that imprisonment for debt never promoted the fulfilment of contracts, nor has its abolition discouraged it.

As for the lower classes, one visit to a prison suffices. There, if you ask a prisoner why the punishment did not deter him from the crime, you generally get no answer, because he has never thought about it. Or else he replies, as I have often found, that "if you were afraid of hurting yourself when you went to work, you would give up working." These indeed are what one would expect to be the feelings prevailing amongst the lower social strata, to whom honest sentiments and ideas, which for us are traditional and organic, come very late--just as Mr. Stanley observed that the people in Central Africa are only now beginning to employ stone guns, which in past ages were used in Europe.

Another fallacy which helps to strengthen confidence in punishments is that the effect of exceptional and summary laws is treated on the same basis as that of the ordinary codes, slow and uncertain in their procedure, which saps all their force by the chance of immunity, and the interval between the unlawful act and its legal consequence.

Lombroso and Tarde, indeed, have confronted me with historic examples of vigorous and even savage repressions, whereby it was possible to stamp out some epidemic crime. But these examples are not conclusive, for I have shown that, as soon as these exceptional repressions were at an end, as, for instance, after the death of Pope Sixtus V., brigandage and other crimes were persistently renewed. But my main rejoinder is this, that these exceptional repressions depend upon the jus belli; and therefore cannot enter into the ordinary and constant methods of penal administration. This may not have the effect of an extraordinary repression, secured by a somewhat unscrupulous promptitude, which strikes innocent and guilty alike; and thus it is impossible to treat as equal, or even to compare, the influence of methods which are essentially different.

Another false comparison is drawn between the effective force of various punishments, and their potentiality is confounded, whereas it is necessary to distinguish the punishment of the written code from that of the judge, and still more from that carried into execution. In fact it is only natural that punishment should more or less terrify the criminal who has been judged and is about to be condemned; but this in no way proves its efficacy, which should have been displayed by the menace of the law in guarding the prisoner against the crime. Even with the death penalty, there are many instances of condemned persons who, through congenital insensibility, submit to it cynically. Moreover, for such as have been overwhelmed with terror when the moment of execution arrived, the utmost that this fact can prove is that they are so constituted as to give themselves up completely to the impression of the moment, without the energy to resist it. In other words, so long as the punishment is distant and uncertain, they were not terrified, but having always yielded to the impression of the moment, they yielded to the criminal impulse.

For other punishments, also, it is known that punitive methods, even when not contrary to the law, as they sometimes are in Italy, are always less stern than simple folk imagine when they read the codes and the sentences. And criminals naturally judge of punishments by their own experience, that is to say, in accordance with their practical application, and not with the more or less candid threats of the lawmaker.

If we add to vindictive feeling, historic traditions, oblivion of bio-psychic differences of the social strata, the confounding of exceptional laws and ordinary punishments, and of the varying effective force of punishment, the attitude of the public mind and the natural tendency of criminalists to think only of their two syllogistic symbols of crime and punishment--if we further add the easy-going idea of the multitude, that the inscribing of a law in the statute-book is a sufficient remedy for social diseases, we can readily understand how this exaggerated and illusory confidence in punishment is so persistent, and crops up in every theoretical or practical discussion, in spite of the strong refutation which is daily afforded by facts and psychological observation.

All human actions, like the actions of animals, are developed between the two opposite poles of pleasure and pain, by the attraction of the former and the repulsion of the latter. And punishment, which is one of the social forms of pain, is always a direct motive in human conduct, as it is also an indirect guide, by virtue of its being a sanction of justice, unconsciously strengthening respect for the law. But still this psychological truth, whilst it demonstrates the natural character of punishment, and the consequent absurdity of abolishing it as absolutely void of efficacy, does not destroy our conclusion as to the slight efficacy of punishment as a counteraction of crime.

We have only to distinguish between punishment as a natural sanction and punishment as a social sanction in order to see how the really great power of natural punishment almost entirely disappears in social punishment, which in all our systems is but a sorry caricature.

The mute but inexorable reaction of nature against every action which infringes her laws, and the grievous consequences which inevitably follow for the man who has infringed them, constitute a repression of the most efficacious kind, wherein every man, especially in the earlier years of his life, receives daily and never to be forgotten lessons. This is the discipline of natural consequence, which is a genuine educational method, long since pointed out by Rousseau, and developed by Spencer and Bain.

But in this natural and spontaneous form, the punishment derives its whole force from the inevitable character of the consequences. And it is one of the few observations of practical psychology which have been made and repeated by the classical students of crime, that in punishment, and especially the punishment of death, the certainty is more effectual than the severity. And I will add that even a small uncertainty takes away from a pain which we fear, much of its repelling force, whereas even a great uncertainty does not destroy the attraction of a pleasure which we are hoping for.

Here, then, we have a primary and potent cause of the slight efficacy of legal punishments, in the picturing of the many chances of escape. First there is the chance of not being detected, which is the most powerful spring of all contemplated crime: then the chance, in case of detection, that the evidence will not be strong enough, that the judges will be merciful, or will be deceived, that judgment may be averted amidst the intricacies of the trial, that clemency may either reverse or mitigate the sentence. These are so many psychological causes which, conflicting with the natural fear of unpleasant consequences, weaken the repellent force of legal punishment, whilst they are unknown to natural punishment.

There is also another psychological condition which, undermining even the force of natural punishment, almost entirely destroys the power of social punishment; and that is improvidence. We see, in fact, that even the most certain natural consequences are defied, and lose most of their power to guard an improvident man from anti-natural and dangerous actions. Now in regard to legal punishment, even apart from passionate impulse, it is known that criminals, occasional and other, are specially improvident, in common with savages and children. This weakness is conspicuous enough in the lower and less instructed classes, but amongst criminals it is a genuine characteristic of psychological infirmity.

Now, whilst a very slight force is sufficient to produce very great and constant effects, when it acts in harmony with natural tendency and environment, every process, on the other hand, which is opposed to the natural tendencies of man, or which does not follow them closely, encounters a resistance which triumphs in the last resort.

Everyday life gives us many examples. The university student, when he gambles, risks on a single card the last remnant of his allowance, and prepares for himself a thousand privations. Miners and workmen at dangerous trades refuse to take warning by the sight of comrades whom they have seen dying or repeatedly attacked by disease. M. Despine related that, during the cholera of 1866, at Bilbao, there were some who set up an imitation of the disease in order to obtain charitable relief, though in several cases death ensued. M. Fayet, in an essay on the statistics of accused persons in France, extending over twenty years, remarked that specific and proportionately greater criminality was displayed by notaries and bailiffs, who knew better than any one else the punishments fixed by law. And in the statistics of capital punishment at Ferrara, during nine centuries, I discovered the significant fact that there is a succession of notaries executed for forgery, frequently at very short intervals, in the same town. This attests the truth of the observation made by Montesquieu and Beccaria, as against the deterrent power of the death penalty, for men grow accustomed to the sight; and this again is confirmed by the fact mentioned by Mr. Roberts, a gaol chaplain, and M. Berenger, a magistrate, that several condemned men had previously been present at executions, and by another fact mentioned by Despine and Angelucci, that in the same town, and often in the same place, in which executions had been carried out, murders are often committed on the same day.

A man does not change his identity; and no penal code, whether mild or severe, can change his natural and invincible tendencies, such as inclination to pleasure and persistent hope of impunity.

Let us also observe that, as Mill said, the permanent efficacy of any measure in the spheres of politics, economy, and administration, is always inversely proportional to its force and suddenness. Now punishment does not stand the test even of this sociological law, for in its essence it is only the primitive reaction of force against force. It is true that, as Beccaria said, the classical school has always aimed at rendering social reaction against crime less violent; but that is not enough. Henceforward, if we are to adapt ourselves to psychological and sociological laws, the development of our defensive administration must tend to render this social reaction less direct. If the struggle for existence is always to remain the supreme law of living creatures, yet it is not necessary that it should always be developed in the violent forms of primitive humanity. On the contrary, one of the results of social progress is to make the struggle for existence less violent and less direct.

In the same way, the continuous struggle between society and criminals, instead of being a physical and social force, directly opposed to a physical individual force, should rather become an indirect system of psychical forces. Penal law in society has the same qualities as education in the family and pedagogy in schools. All the three were once dominated by the idea of taming human passions by force; the rod was supreme. In course of time it was perceived that this produced unexpected results, such as violence and hypocrisy, and then men thought fit to modify their punishments. But in our own days schoolmasters see the advantage of relying solely on the free play of tendencies and bio- psychological laws. Similarly the defensive function of society, as Romagnosi said, in place of being a physical and repressive system, ought to be a moral and preventive system, based on the natural laws of biology, psychology, and sociology.

Force is always a bad remedy for force. In the Middle Ages, when punishments were brutal, crimes were equally savage; and society, in demoralising rivalry with the atrocity of criminals, laboured in a vicious circle. Now, in the lower social grades, the brutal man, who often resorts to violence, is in his turn frequently the victim of violence; so that, amongst criminals, a scar is somewhat of a professional distinction.

To sum up, our doctrine as to the efficacy of punishments does not consist, as some critics too sparing of their arguments have maintained, in an absolute negation, but rather and especially in objecting to the traditional prejudice that punishments are the best and most effectual remedies of crime.

What we say is this. Punishment by itself, as a means of repression, possesses a negative rather than a positive value; not only because it has not the same influence on all anthropological types of criminals, but also because its use is rather to preclude the serious mischief which would result from impunity than to convert, as some imagine that it can, an anti-social into a social being. But impunity would lead to a demoralisation of the popular conscience in regard to crimes and offences, to an increase of the profound lack of foresight in criminals, and to the removal of the present impediment to fresh crimes during the term of incarceration.

It is the same with education, the modifying power of which is commonly exaggerated. Education, though it has an enduring influence on children, and is therefore more effectual than punishment, is far more serviceable in eliminating anti-social tendencies, whereof we all possess the germs, than in any supposed creation of social tendencies and forces which were not present from birth.

Thus, whilst the consequences of impunity and lack of education are serious and mischievous, still this does not prove conversely that punishment and education have in reality so positive an influence as is commonly attributed to them.

It is precisely on the ground of this negative, yet real efficacy of punishments, especially whilst they are being carried out, that, whilst we appreciate the mitigation of punitive discipline which has been achieved by the classical school, we believe, on the other hand, that their abbreviation of the term of punishments is altogether mistaken and dangerous. We admit that punishment ought not to be an arbitrary and inhuman torture, and for this reason we have no sympathy with the system of solitary confinement, now so much in fashion with the classical jurists and prison authorities, precisely because it is inhuman, as well as unwise and needlessly expensive.

It is a psychological absurdity and a social danger, which nevertheless underlies the new Italian penal code, that punishment ought to consist more and more in a short isolation of the prisoner. For, setting aside the well-known results of short punishments, such as corruption and recidivism, it is evident that in this way punishment is deprived of its main element of negative efficiency against crime, as well as of its effect in preventing crime during the incarceration of the criminal.

II.

Since punishments, instead of being the simple panacea of crime which popular opinion, encouraged by the opinions of classical writers on crime and of legislators, imagine them, are very limited in their deterrent influence, it is natural that the criminal sociologist should look for other means of social defence in the actual study of crimes and of their natural origin.

We are taught by the everyday experience of the family, the school, associations of men and women, and the history of social life, that in order to lessen the danger of outbreaks of passion it is more useful to take them in their origin, and in flank, than to meet them when they have gathered force.

Bentham relates that in England the delays caused by hard-drinking couriers, who used to be heavily fined without any good result, were obviated by combining passenger traffic with the postal service. Employers of labour secure industry and the most productive work far more easily by offering a share of the realised profits than by a system of fines. In the German universities, academic jealousies and intolerance have been in great measure overcome by paying the professors in proportion to the number of their pupils, so that the Faculties find it to their interest to engage and encourage the best professors, in order to attract as many students as possible. Thus the activity and zeal of professors, magistrates, and officials would be stimulated if their remuneration depended not only on the automatic test of seniority, but also on the progress displayed by publications, sentences not reversed, settlements not cancelled, and the like. It is better to regulate the disturbing restlessness of children by timely diversions rather than by attempting to repress them in a manner injurious to their physical and moral health. So in lunatic asylums and prisons, work is a better means of order and discipline than chains and castigation. In brief, we obtain more from men by consulting their self-respect and interests than by threats and restraint

If the counteraction of punishment must inevitably be opposed to criminal activity, still it is more conducive to social order to prevent or diminish this activity by means of an indirect and more effective force.

In the economic sphere, it has been observed that when a staple product fails, recourse is had to less esteemed substitutes, in order to supply the natural wants of mankind. So in the criminal sphere, as we are convinced by experience that punishments are almost devoid of deterrent effect, we must have recourse to the best available substitutes for the purpose of social defence.

These methods of indirect defence I have called penal substitutes. But whereas the food substitutes are as a rule only secondary products, brought into temporary use, penal substitutes should become the main instruments of the function of social defence, for which punishments will come to be secondary means, albeit permanent. For in this connection we must not forget the law of criminal saturation, which in every social environment makes a minimum of crime inevitable, on account of the natural factors inseparable from individual and social imperfection. Punishments in one form or another will always be, for this minimum, the ultimate though not very profitable remedy against outbreaks of criminal activity.

These penal substitutes, when they have once been established in the conscience and methods of legislators, through the teaching of criminal sociology, will be the recognised form of treatment for the social factors of crime. And they will also be more possible and practical than that universal social metamorphosis, direct and uncompromising, insisted on by generous but impatient reformers, who scorn these substitutes as palliatives because humanitarian enthusiasm causes them to forget that social organisms, like animal organisms, can be only partially and gradually transformed.

The idea of these penal substitutes amounts, in short, to this. The legislator, observing the origins, conditions, and effects of individual and collective activity, comes to recognise their psychological and sociological laws, whereby he will be able to obtain a mastery over many of the factors of crime, and especially over the social factors, and thus secure an indirect but more certain influence over the development of crime. That is to say, in all legislative, political, economic, administrative, and penal arrangements, from the greatest institutions to the smallest details, the social organism will be so adjusted that human activity, instead of being continually and unprofitably menaced with repression, will be insensibly directed into non-criminal channels, leaving free scope for energy and the satisfaction of individual needs, under conditions least exposed to violent disturbance or occasions of law-breaking.

It is just this fundamental idea of penal substitutes which shows how necessary it is that the sociologist and legislator should have such a preparation in biology and psychology as Mr. Spencer justly insisted on in his ``Introduction to Social Science.'' And it is the fundamental idea rather than the substitutes themselves that we should bear in mind if we would realise their theoretical and practical value as part of a system of criminal sociology.

As for the efficacy of any particular penal substitute, I readily admit, in some sense at least, the partial criticisms which have been passed upon them. Apart from such as simply say that they do not believe in the use of alternatives to punishment, and such as confine themselves to the futile question whether this theory belongs to criminal science or to police administration, a majority of criminal sociologists have now definitely accepted the doctrine of penal substitutes. This theory is accepted, not as an absolute panacea of crime, but, as I have always stated it, in the sense of a combination of measures analogous to penal repression; in place of trusting solely to repression for the defence of society against crime.

Let us take note of a few examples.

I. In the Economic Sphere.--Free Trade (apart from the temporary necessity of protecting a particular manufacturing or agricultural industry), by preventing famines and exceptional high prices of and taxes on food, eliminates many crimes and offences, especially against property.--Unrestricted emigration is a safety- valve, especially for a country in which this phenomenon, assuming large proportions, carries off many persons who are easily driven to crime by wretchedness, or by their unbalanced energy. Thus the number of recidivists has diminished in Ireland, not by virtue of her prison systems, but by emigration, which reached forty-six per cent. of released prisoners. In Italy, also, there has been a decrease of crime since 1880, owing to other causes, such as mild winters and plentiful harvests, but also through a vast increase of emigration.--Smuggling, which for centuries resisted extremely harsh punishments, such as amputation of the hand, and even death, and which still resists prison and the fire-arms of the revenue officers, is suppressed by the lowering of the import tariff, as M. Villerme has shown in the case of France. So that everyday facts justify the system of Adam Smith, who said that the law which punished smuggling, after creating the temptation, and which increased the punishment when it increased the temptation, was opposed to all justice; whilst Bentham, on the contrary, departing from his maxim that the punishment ought to be dreaded more strongly than the offence attracted, called for the stern repression of smuggling.--The system of taxation which touches wealth and visible resources instead of the prime necessaries of life, and which is proportional to the taxpayer's income, diminishes the systematic frauds which no punishment availed to stop, and it will also abolish the arbitrary and exaggerated fiscal traditions which have been the cause of rebellions and outrages. In fact, Fregier describes the criminal industries which are called into existence by octrois, and which will disappear with the abolition of these absurd and unjust duties. And whilst M. Allard demonstrated that a decrease of taxes on necessaries would have beneficial effects, not only in economic affairs but also in respect of commercial frauds, the Report on French Criminal Statistics for 1872 calmly continued to call for more severe repression of such frauds. To this M. Mercier replied that if the cause--that is to say, disproportionate taxes--were not removed, it would be impossible to prevent the effects.--Immunity from taxation for the minimum necessary to existence, by preventing distraint, and the consequent diminution of small properties, which means the increase of the very poor, will obviate many crimes, as we see from the agrarian conditions in Ireland. Thus there is a demand in Italy for the inalienability of small properties, as in America under the Homestead Exemption Law.--Public works, during famine and hard winters, check the increase of crimes against property, the person, and public order. For instance, during the scarcity of 1853-5 in France, there was no such enormous increase of theft as during the famine of 1847, simply because the Government set up vast relief works in the winter months.

The taxes and other indirect restrictions on the production and sale of alcohol are far more efficacious than our more or less enormous gaols. The question of pronounced and chronic drunkenness has increased in gravity, owing to its effect upon the physical and moral health of the people.

In France the average consumption of wine, estimated at 62 litres (13.64 gallons) per head in 1829, exceeded 100 litres in 1869; and in Paris the average of 120 litres in 1819-30, reached 227 litres in 1881. The average yearly consumption of alcohol in France rose from .93 in 1829 to 3.24 in 1872, and 3.9 in 1885, the rates in a few towns being still higher. The total manufacture of alcohol in France (95 per cent. of which is consumed in the form of drink) rose from 479,680 hectolitres in 1843 to 1,309,565 in 1879, and 2,004,000 in 1887. Simultaneously, we have seen that there was an increase of crimes and offences in France, suicides in particular having increased from 1,542 in 1829 to 8,202 in 1887.

Moreover I have shown by a special table (Archivio di Psichiatria) that in France, despite a certain inevitable variation from year to year, there is a manifest correspondence of increase and decrease between the number of homicides, assaults, and malicious wounding, and the more or less abundant vintage, especially in the years of extraordinary variations, whether of failure of the vintage (1853-5, 1859, 1867, 1873, 1878-80), attended by a remarkable diminution of crime (assaults and wounding), or of abundant vintages (1850, 1856-8, 1862-3, 1865, 1868, 1874-5) attended by an increase of crime.

I was also the first to show that in the vintage months there is an increase of occasional crimes and offences against the person, owing to that connection between drink and crime which had already been remarked upon by M. Pierquin amongst others, and illustrated by the newspaper reporters on the days which follow Sundays and holidays.

But apart from their natural variation, the connection between drink and crime is definitely established. Every day we have the confirmation of Morel's statement, that ``alcoholism has produced a demoralised and brutalised class of wretched beings, characterised by an early depravation of instincts, and by indulgence in the most immoral and dangerous actions." It is useless to quote again in this place the data of psycho- pathology and legal medicine, or those of prison statistics relating to imprisoned drunkards, or to tavern brawls as the proved causes of crime.

Nevertheless it is a fact that the relation of cause and effect between drink and crime has recently been denied, with the aid of arguments based upon statistics. M. Tammeo opened the discussion by observing that the countries of Europe and the provinces of Italy distinguished by the largest consumption of alcohol, show lower ratios under the worst crimes of violence. He gave to his remark a relative and limited value, for he only denied that the abuse of liquor was the most active cause of crime. After him M. Fournier de Flaix, maintaining the same proposition with the same statistical arguments, and admitting that ``alcohol is a special scourge for the individual who indulges in it," yet concluded that ``alcoholism is not a scourge which menaces the European race." And he repeated that the nations which consumed the greatest quantity of alcohol show a slighter frequency of crime, especially against the person. Lastly M. Colajanni enlarged upon the same proposition, using the statistical data so fully set out by M. Kummer, and drew a still more positive conclusion, that ``there is a lack of constancy, regularity, and universality in the relations, coincidence, and sequence, as between alcoholism and crime and suicide;

so that it is impossible to establish any statistical relation of cause and effect between these phenomena."

Passing over the grave errors of fact in M. Colajanni's brochure, I will only observe that this proposition is a pure misapprehension of statistical logic.

If we once admit (and unfortunately it cannot be denied) the bad influence of alcohol on bodily and mental health, in the form of spirits as well as of wine--as to which it is not correct to say that the southern departments are not consumers of alcohol--it cannot be maintained that alcohol, which is physically and morally injurious to individuals, is not hurtful to nations, which are but aggregates of individuals.

There is an easy answer to the statistical arguments. (1) A symmetrical and continuous agreement of figures is never found in any collection of statistics, for in all that concerns a society the intervention of individual, physical, and social causes is inevitable. (2) A negative conclusion from these partial and natural disagreements (for it is especially true in biology and sociology that every rule has its exceptions, due to intervening causes) would only be justified if it had been maintained that alcoholism is the sole and exclusive cause of crime. But as this has never been asserted by anybody, all the statistical arguments of Fournier and Colajanni are based on a misapprehension. And unfortunately they do not destroy the link of causality between drink and crime. This connection is occasional, in assaults, wounding, and homicide in acute alcoholism. It is habitual, in the case of chronic alcoholism, as in crimes against property, the person, morality, and public officers. And this in spite of the relatively low figures, though lower than the facts warrant, contained in the general statements, apart from special and scientific inquiries into alcoholism as a direct and manifest cause of crime and suicide.

I wrote as early as 1881 that alcoholism, prior to its becoming a cause, is the effect of wretched social conditions in the poorer classes; and that to the one-sided simplicity of economic causes it is necessary to add certain bio-psychical conditions and conditions of physical environment, which go far to determine the geographical distribution of spirit-alcoholism (chronic and more serious, in northern countries and provinces) and wine-alcoholism (acute and less deep-seated, in the countries and provinces of the south).

It was therefore natural that indirect measures against alcoholism should have been resorted to long ago, such as the raising of the tax on alcoholic drinks, and the lowering of that on wholesome beverages, such as coffee, tea, and beer; strict limitation of the number of licenses; increased responsibility of license-holders before the law, as in America; the expulsion of tipsy members from workmen's societies; the provision of cheap and wholesome amusements; the testing of wines and spirits for adulteration; better organised and combined temperance societies;

the circulation of tracts on the injurious effects of alcohol; the abolition of certain festivals which tended rather to demoralisation than to health; discouragement of the custom of paying wages on Saturday; the establishment of voluntary temperance homes, as in America, England, and Switzerland.

North America, England, Sweden and Norway, France, Belgium, Holland, and Switzerland have applied remedies against drunkenness (to the length of a State monopoly of drink in Switzerland); but with too much zeal for public revenue, and, under the pretext of public health, almost exclusively framed with a view to duties on manufacture, distribution, and consumption. Yet these duties are quite inadequate by themselves, and may even tend to the injury of the physical and moral health of the nation, the increase of price, leading to frauds and adulteration.

Penal laws against drunkenness, naturally resorted to in all countries, are far from being effectual. There is so far no system of direct and indirect measures against alcoholism, duly co-ordinated, beyond taxation and punishment. And we perceive, as for instance in France, in spite of the repressive law introduced by my distinguished friend Senator Roussel (January, 1873), and in spite of the extremely high duties, which were doubled in 1872 and 1880, that alcoholism persists with a terrible and fatal increase. So it is, more or less, in every country still, in spite of duties and punishments.

The irregularity of wages, and the deceitful vigour imparted by the first recourse to alcohol, the poverty and excessive toil of the working classes, insufficiency of food, inherited habits, and the lack of efficacious preventive measures, are influences which prevent the working man from resisting this scourge; and no fiscal or repressive law, acting solely by direct compulsion, will ever be able to paralyse these natural tendencies, which can only be weakened by indirect measures. On the other hand, when we remember that habitual intoxication, so common in mediaeval days amongst the nobles and townsfolk, has grown less and less frequent in those classes (aided by the introduction and rapid diffusion of coffee since the time of Louis XIV.), it is possible to hope that the improvement of economic, intellectual, and moral conditions amongst the populace will gradually succeed in modifying this terrible plague of drink, which cannot be cured all at once.

To continue our illustrations of penal substitutes, we see that the substitution of metallic money for a paper medium decreases the number of forgers, who on the contrary had defied penal servitude for life. False money is more easily detected than a spurious note.[14]--Money dealers and dealers in precious stones have done more than any punishment to check the crime of usury, as was shown in the case of Spain, after her American conquests; whereas mediaeval punishments never prevented the recrudescence of usury in one form or another. Popular and Agricultural Credit Banks, which are practically within the reach of all, are more efficacious against usury in our own days than the special repressive laws enacted once more in

Germany and Austria, under the influence of the old illusion.--With the diminution of interest on the public funds the stream of capital has been diverted into commerce, manufactures, and agriculture, thus warding off stagnation, with the bankruptcies, forgeries, frauds, &c., which result therefrom.--The adjustment of salaries to the needs of public officials, and to general economic conditions, stems the tide of corruption and embezzlement, which were partly due to their concealed poverty.-- Limited hours of duty for the responsible services on which the safety of the public depends, as for instance in railway stations, are far more serviceable in preventing accidents than the useless punishment of those who are guilty of manslaughter.-- High-roads, railways, and tramways disperse predatory bands in rural districts, just as wide streets and large and airy dwellings, with public lighting and the destruction of slums, prevent robbery with violence, concealment of stolen goods, and indecent assaults.--Inspection of workshops and shorter hours for children's labour, with their superintendence of married women, may be a check on indecent assaults, which penal servitude does not prevent.--Cheap workmen's dwellings, and general sanitary measures for houses both in urban and rural districts, care being taken not to crowd them with poor families, tend to physical health, as well as to prevent many forms of immorality.--Co-operative and mutual societies, provident societies and insurance against old age, funds for sick and infirm workmen, employers' liability for accidents during work, from machinery or otherwise; popular savings' banks, charity organisation societies and the like, obviate a large number of offences against property and the person much better than a penal code.--I have maintained in the Italian Parliament that the reform of religious charities, which in Italy represent funds to the amount of two milliards, might lead to the prevention of crime.-- Measures for the discouragement of mendacity and vagrancy, above all agricultural colonies, as in Holland, Belgium, Germany, and Austria, would be the best penal substitute for the very frequent offences committed by vagabonds. Thus it may be concluded that a prudent social legislation, not stopping short at mere superficial and perfunctory reforms, might constitute a genuine code of penal substitutes, which could be set against the mass of criminal impulses engendered by the wretched conditions of the most numerous classes of society.

[14] Coiners and forgers of notes constitute .09 per cent. of the total of condemned persons in France, and .04 per cent. in Belgium; but they reach .4 per cent. in Italy, on account of the greater circulation of banknotes.

II. In the Political Sphere.--For the prevention of political crime, such as assassination, rebellion, conspiracies, civil war, arbitrary repression and prevention by the police are powerless; there is no other means than harmony between the Government and the national aspirations. Italy has been a conspicuous example of this, for under the rule of the foreigner, neither the scaffold nor the galleys could hinder political outrages, which have disappeared with national independence. So with Ireland and Russia. Germany, which believed that it could stamp out socialism by exceptional penal laws, discovered its mistake.--For so-called press offences (which are either ordinary offences committed by the aid of the press, or are not offences at all), nothing but freedom of opinion can render attacks and provocations of a political type less frequent.--Respect for the law spreads through a nation by the example on the part of the governing classes and authorities of constant respect for the rights of individuals and associations, far better than by policemen and prisons.--Electoral reform adapted to the condition of a country is the only remedy against electoral offences.--Similarly, in addition to the economic reforms already indicated, political and parliamentary reforms are much more serviceable than the penal code in preventing many offences of a social and political type, provided that a more real harmony has been established between a country and its lawful representation, and that the latter is freed from the occasions and the forms which lead to its abuse, by removing technical questions from injurious political influences, and giving the people a more direct authority over public affairs, including the referendum.--Finally, that great mass of crimes, isolated or epidemic, evolved by unsatisfied needs and the neglect of separate divisions of a country, which differ in climate, race, traditions, language, customs, and interests, would be largely eliminated if we were to dispense with the vague folly of political symmetry and bureaucratic centralisation, and in their place to adapt the laws to the special features of the respective localities. National unity in no way depends upon legislative and administrative uniformity, which is merely its unhealthy exaggeration. It is indeed inevitable that laws, which in our day merely represent a mode of contact between the most varied moral, social and economic conditions of different localities, should always be inadequate to social needs--too restricted and slow in action for one part of the country, too sweeping and premature for another part, just as the average convict's garb is too long for those who are short, and too short for those who are tall. Administrative federation with political unity (e pluribus unum) would furnish us with an aggregate of penal substitutes, restoring to each part of the social organism that freedom of movement and development which is a universal law of biology and sociology--for an organism is but a federation too lightly appreciated by the advocates of an artificial uniformity, such as ends by conflicting with unity itself.

III. In the Scientific Sphere.--The development of science, which creates fresh instruments of crime, such as fire-arms, the press, photography, lithography, new poisons, dynamite, electricity, hypnotism, and so forth, sooner or later provides the antidote also, which is more efficacious than penal repression.-- The press, anthropometric photography of prisoners, telegraphy, railways, are powerful auxiliaries against crime.--Dissection and the progress of toxicology have decreased the number of poisoning cases; and experience has already proved that ``Marsh's preparation'' has rendered poisoning by arsenic, once so common, comparatively rare.--A similar process has recently been suggested as a means of detection in cases of forgery, for when documents are exposed to iodine vapour, effaced or altered writing is restored.--Women doctors will diminish the opportunities of immorality.-- The free expression of opinion will do more to prevent its possible dangers than trials of a more or less scandalous kind.--Piracy, which was not extirpated by punishments which are now obsolete, is disappearing under the effects of steam navigation.--The spread of Malthusian ideas prevents abortion and infanticides.

72

[15]--Systematic bookkeeping, by its clearness and simplicity, obviates many frauds and embezzlements, which were encouraged by the old complicated methods.-- Cheques, by avoiding the necessity of frequent conveyance of money, do more to prevent theft than punishments can do.--The credentials given by some banks to their clerks, whose duty it is to witness the signature of the actual debtor, prevent the falsification of bills.--Certain bankers have adopted the practice of taking an instantaneous photograph of every one presenting cheques for large amounts.-- Safes, bolts, and alarm- bells, are a great security against thieves. --As a preventive of murder in railway carriages, it has been found that alarm signals and methods of securing the carriage-doors from the inside, are more effectual than penal codes.

[15] No doubt there may be a difference of opinion on this subject in France, where public opinion is too much exercised over the problem of depopulation. I agree with M. Varigny (``La Theorie du Nombre," Revue des Deux Mondes, Dec. 15, 1890) that the population of a country is not the sole, or even the principal consideration. Apart from physical characteristics (race), intellectual and moral qualities, and the productiveness of the soil on which M. Varigny dwells, we must take into account, as it seems to me, the unquestionable law by virtue of which the struggle for existence, amongst individuals as amongst nations, becomes gradually less vehement and direct. War, which is an everyday matter with savages, grows constantly more rare and difficult. The varying social and international conscience of civilised humanity is not to be neglected, and it must be reckoned with as a positive factor in considering the destiny of nations. Men continue to speak of the perils of war (in which numbers stand for a great deal, but are not the exclusive element) as though the social conscience of our own day were still the same as that of the Middle Ages. In several respects, on the other hand, the thinner population of France is one cause of its wealth, and therefore of its power. Germany has a more numerous, but also a poorer population. And I do not believe that the actual power of nations, on which their future depends, consists in loading a people with arms after enfeebling it by military expenditure, which from the year 1880 has indicated a distinct epidemic mania on the continent of Europe.

IV. In the Legislative and Administrative Sphere.--Wise testamentary legislation prevents murders through the impatient greed of next-of-kin, as in France during a former age, with what was known as ``succession powder."--A law to facilitate the securing of paternal assent for the marriage of children (as suggested by Herschel in his ``Theory of Probabilities") in countries which require the assent of both parents, and for affiliation and breach of promise of marriage, with provision for children born out of wedlock, are excellent as against concubinage, infanticide, abortion, exposure of infants, indecent assaults, and murders by women abandoned after seduction. On this head Bentham said that concubinage regulated by civil laws would be less mischievous than that which the law does not recognise but cannot prevent.--Cheap and easy law is a preventive of crimes and offences against public order, the person and property, as I have already said.--The ancient Italian institution of Advocate of the Poor, if substituted for the present illusory assistance by the courts, would prevent many acts of revenge. So also would a strict and speedy indemnity for the victims of other men's crimes, intrusted to a public minister when the injured person is not able to resort to the law; for as I have maintained, with the approval of sundry criminal sociologists, civil responsibility for crime ought to be as much a social obligation as penal responsibility, and not a mere private concern.--Simplification of the law would prevent a large number of frauds, contraventions, &c., for, apart from the metaphysical and ironical assertion that ignorance of the law excuses no man, it is certain that our forest of codes, laws, decrees, regulations and so forth, leads to endless misapprehensions and mistakes, and therefore to contraventions and offences.--Commercial laws on the civil responsibility of directors, on bankruptcy proceedings and the registration of shareholders, on bankrupts' discharges, on industrial and other exchanges, would do more than penal servitude to prevent fraudulent bankruptcy.--Courts of honour, recognised and regulated by law, would obviate duels without having recourse to more or less serious punishments.--A well organised system of conveyancing checks forgery and fraud, just as registration offices have almost abolished the palming and repudiation of children, which were so common in mediaeval times. Deputy Michelin, in order to discourage bigamy, proposed in 1886 to institute in the registers of births for every commune a special column for the civil standing of each individual, so that any one who contemplated marriage would have to produce a certificate from this register, and thus would be unable to conceal a previous marriage which had not been dissolved by death or divorce.--The form of indictment by word of mouth in penal procedure has prevented many calumnies and false charges.--Foundling and orphan homes, or, still better, some less old-fashioned substitute, such as lying-in hospitals and home attendance for young mothers, might do much to prevent infanticide and abortion, which are not checked by the severest punishment.--Prisoners' aid societies, especially for the young, might be useful as penal substitutes, although much less so than is generally alleged, with plenty of eloquence and little practical work. There is always this strong objection to them, that we ought to succour workmen who continue honest in spite of their wretchedness before those who have been in prison; and again, in place of bestowing patronage on released prisoners without distinction, many of whom are incorrigible, we ought to select the occasional criminals and criminals of passion, who alone are capable of amendment; and assisting them we should avoid anything like police formalities. As a matter of fact it appears that, even in England, where these societies are most active, their intervention, like all direct charity, is too far below the needs of those for whom provision is necessary.

V. In the Sphere of Education.--It has been proved that mere book education, whilst it is useful in rendering certain gross frauds more difficult, in extending a knowledge of the laws, and above all in diminishing improvidence, so characteristic of the occasional criminal, is far from being the panacea of crime which people imagined when they found in the criminal statistics a large proportion of illiterate prisoners. It must also be said that schools which are not closely inspected are frequently hotbeds of immorality. It is necessary, therefore, to rely on the influence of a wider education, limited though this may be in its turn. I do not mean a mechanical instruction in moral maxims, appealing to the intelligence without reaching the feelings, but rather of the examples afforded by every kind of social institution, by the government and the press, by the school of the stage and of public entertainments.--It would be well, however, to abolish certain vulgar and sensual entertainments, and to substitute for them wholesome amusements and exercises, public baths, properly superintended, and so built as to render private meetings impossible, cheap theatres, and so forth. Thus the prohibition of cruel spectacles, and the suppression of gambling houses, are excellent penal substitutes.--The experimental method in the teaching of children, which applies the laws of physio-psychology, according to the physical and moral type of each pupil, and by giving him less of archaeology, and more knowledge serviceable in actual life, by the mental discipline of the natural sciences, which alone can develop in him a sense of the actual, such as our classical schools only enfeeble, would adapt men better for the struggle of existence, whilst diminishing the number of those left without occupation, who are the candidates of crime.--Many of the causes of crime would be nipped in the bud by checking degeneration through physical education of the young, as well as by preventing demoralisation by means of the education of abandoned children, at such institutions as the workhouse, ragged and industrial schools, so well developed in England--or, still better, by the boarding out of children, so as to avoid over- crowding.--One class of inducements to crime would be eliminated by restrictions imposed on scandalous publications which concern themselves exclusively with crime, having no other object than to trade upon the most brutal passions, and which are allowed to exist under an abstract conception of liberty, save that the responsible conductors are punished when the evil has been done.--Similarly there ought to be some restriction upon the right of admission to police-courts and assizes, where our women hustle each other as the Roman women of the decline scrambled to be present at the imperial circus-shows, and where our young men and our hardened criminals receive lessons in the art of committing crimes with greater smartness and precaution.

The instances which I have given, and which might be multiplied into a preventive code as long as the penal code, prove to demonstration how large a part is played by social factors in the genesis of crime, and especially of occasional crime. But they prove still more clearly that the legislator, by modifying these causes, can influence the development of crime within limits imposed by the competition of other anthropological and physical factors. Quetelet was right, therefore, when he said in this connection, ``Since the crimes committed every year seem to be the necessity of our social organisation, and their number cannot be diminished if the causes to which they are due cannot be modified in a preventive sense, it behoves legislators to recognise these causes, and to eliminate them as far as possible. They must frame the budget of crime as they frame that of the national revenue and expenditure."

It must nevertheless be borne in mind that all this will have to be done apart from the penal code; for it is true, however strange, that history, statistics, and direct observation of criminal phenomena prove that penal laws are the least effectual in preventing crime, whilst the strongest influence is exercised by laws of the economic, political, and administrative order.

In conclusion, the legislator should be convinced by the teaching of scientific observation that social reforms are much more serviceable than the penal code in preventing an inundation of crime. The legislator, on whom it devolves to preserve the health of the social organism, ought to imitate the physician, who preserves the health of the individual by the aid of experimental science, resorts as little as possible, and only in extreme cases, to the more forcible methods of surgery, has a limited confidence in the problematic efficiency of medicines, and relies rather on the trustworthy processes of hygienic science. Only then will he be able to avoid the dangerous fallacy, ever popular and full of life, which Signor Vacca, Keeper of the Seals, expressed in these words: ``The less we have recourse to preventive measures, the more severe ought our repression to be." Which is like saying that when a convalescent has no soup to pick up his strength, we ought to administer a drastic drug.

It is precisely on this point that the practical, rather than the merely theoretical, differences between the positive and the classical schools of penal law become evident. Whilst we believe that social reforms and other measures suggested by a study of the natural factors of crime are most effective in preventing crime, legislators, employing the a priori method of the classical school, have for many years past been discussing proposed penal codes, whilst they permit criminality to make steady progress. It is another case of Dum Romae consulitur, Saguntum expugnatur.

And when the legislators find their Byzantine discussions on the ``juridical entities" of crime and punishment broken in upon by a recrudescence of crime, or by a serious manifestation of some phenomenon of social pathology, then all they can do in their perplexity and astonishment is to pass some new repressive law, which for a moment stills the outcry of public opinion, and remits the matter once more from the acute to the chronic phase.

The positive theory of penal substitutes, apart from any particular example, aims precisely at furnishing a mental discipline for legislators, and bringing home to them the duty of constant reinforcements of social prevention, no matter how difficult it may be, before the evil comes to a head, and forces them too late to a course of repression which is as easy as it is fallacious. No doubt it is vexatious and difficult, even in private life, to be perpetually living up to rules of health; and it is easier, if more dangerous, to forget them, and to fly, when the mischief declares itself, to drugs which are too frequently deceptive; but it is just the want of forethought, both public and private, which it is so important to overcome. And as hygienic science was not possible as a theory or as a practice until after the experimental observations and physio-pathology on the causes of disease, especially of epidemic and infectious diseases, together with the discoveries of M. Pasteur, who created bacteriology; so social hygiene as against crime was only possible as a theory, and will not be so as a practice, till the diffusion of the facts of biology and criminal sociology relating to the natural causes of crime, especially of occasional crime.

The great thing is to be convinced that, for social defence against crime, as for the moral elevation of the masses of men, the least measure of progress with reforms which prevent crime is a hundred times more useful and profitable than the publication of an entire penal code.

When a minister introduces a law, for instance, on railways, customs duties, wages, taxation, companies, civil or commercial institutions, there are few who think of the effect which these laws will have on the criminality of the nation, for it is imagined that sufficient has been done in this respect by means of reforms in the penal code. In the social organism, on the other hand, as in individuals, there is an inevitable solidarity, though frequently concealed, between the most distant and different parts.

It is just from these laws of social physiology and pathology that we derive the notion of penal substitutes, which at the same time we must not dissociate from the law of criminal saturation. For if it is true that by modifying the social factors we can produce an effect on the development of crime, and especially of occasional crime, it is also true, unfortunately, that in every social environment there is always a minimum of inevitable criminality, due to the influence of the other factors, biological and physical. Otherwise we might easily fall into the opposite and equally fallacious illusion of thinking that we could absolutely suppress all crimes and offences. For it is easy to reach on one side the empiric idea of penal terrorism, and on the other side the hasty and one-sided conclusion that to abolish some particular institution would get rid of its abuses. The fact is that we must consider before all things whether it is not a less evil to put up with institutions, however inconvenient, and to reform them, than to forfeit all the advantages which they afford. And it must above all be borne in mind that as society cannot exist without law, so law cannot exist without offences against the law. The struggle for existence may be fought by honest or economic activity, or by dishonest and criminal activity. The whole problem is to reduce to a minimum the more or less criminal rufflings and shocks, yet without disturbing ``social order,'' amidst the indifference or servility of a spiritless people, or resorting to policemen and prisons on every slight occasion.

These general observations on penal substitutes in connection with the law of criminal saturation are a sufficient answer to the two chief objections raised even by such as agree with me in theory.

It has been urged, in effect, that some of the penal substitutes which I have enumerated have already been applied, without preventing crime; and again, that there were some institutions which it would be absurd to abolish because the removal of a prohibition would also remove the contravention.

The aim of penal substitutes is not to render all crimes and offences impossible, but only to reduce them to the least possible number in any particular physical and social environment. There are crimes of piracy to this day, but the use of steam in navigation has, none the less, been more effectual than all the penal codes. Murders still occur, though very rarely, on the railways; but it is none the less true that the substitution of the railways and tramways for the old diligences and stage coaches has decimated highway robberies, with or without murder. Divorce does not eliminate wife-murder as a consequence of adultery, but it diminishes its frequency. Similarly, after the protection which is afforded to abandoned children, we shall not be able to close the tribunals through the absence of crimes and offences, but it is certain that the supply of these will be notably diminished.

As for the second objection, I was careful to say, in regard to existing institutions, that we must naturally consider whether the evil arising from violating them or that which would be due to their suppression is the greater. But my main contention is that by reforming these institutions we can do more to prevent crime than by leaving them as they happen to be, or at most granting them the fallacious protection of one or two articles in the penal code.

I will myself add a criticism of the theory of penal substitutes, and it is that they are difficult of application. We have only to think of the immense force of inertia in the habits, traditions and interests which have to be overcome before we can secure the application, not of all, but of any one of the penal substitutes which I have enumerated. And some of these are not simple, or based on a single principle, but comprise an assemblage of co-ordinated reforms, like the prevention of drunkenness, the protection of abandoned children, the accessibility of justice, and so forth.

But if legislators must take into account the actual conditions of the people, and adapt themselves to conditions of time and place, it is the business of science to indicate the goal, however distant and difficult to reach. The first condition of attaining legislative and social reforms is that they should impress themselves beforehand on the public conscience; and this is not possible if science, in spite of transitory difficulties, does not resolutely open up the road which has to be travelled, without any compromise with eclecticism, which means for science what hybridism means for organic life.

Two other objections may be made on the ground of principle to what has been said. The first is that this system of penal substitutes is only the familiar process of prevention of crime. The second is that the criminal expert need not concern himself with it, since prevention is only a question of good government, which has nothing to do with the study of crimes and punishments.

My answer to the second objection is that the importance of taking measures to prevent crime has certainly been dwelt upon, especially from the time of Montesquieu and Beccaria, but it has been only by way of platonic and isolated declaration, with no such systematic development as might have given them practical application, based on experimental observations. Moreover, this prevention has always been held as subsidiary to repression, whereas we have arrived at the positive conclusion that prevention, instead of being a mere secondary aid, should henceforth become the primary defensive function of society, since repression has but an infinitesimal influence upon criminality.

Furthermore, it is important to observe the profound distinction between ordinary prevention and penal substitutes; or in other words, between prevention by police and prevention by society. The former merely seeks to prevent crime when its germ is already developed and active, and it nearly always employs methods of direct coercion, which, being themselves repressive in their character, are often inefficacious, even if they do not provoke additional offences. Social prevention, on the other hand, begins with the original sources of crime, attacking its biological, physical, and social factors, by methods which are wholly indirect, and which rest upon the free play of psychological and sociological laws.

Science, as well as the making of laws, has hitherto been too much influenced by a preference for repression, or at least for administrative police prevention. ``There have been authoritative works and learned folios,'' says Ellero, ``which dealt not only with punishment, but also with torture; there has been none dealing with the provision of means for providing an alternative to punishment.''

After the general observations of Montesquieu, Filangieri, Beccaria, and more recently Tissot, on the influence of religion, climate, soil, and the form of government, upon the penal system rather than the prevention of crime, the authors who studied prevention with wider and more systematic views (excluding the criminal sociologists who have more or less taken the positive point of view), are Bentham, Romagnosi, Barbacovi, Carmignani, Ellero, Lombroso, and a few Englishmen, who, without making much of the theory, have made many practical suggestions of preventive reform. But even these writers either confine themselves to general synthetic considerations, like Romagnosi and Carmignani, or else, entering the domain of facts, and even accepting the idea of social prevention, have made too little of those physio- psychological laws as the natural factors of crime, which alone can furnish a method of regulating human activity. And, when all is said and done, they have clung to punishment as the chief method of prevention.

Hence their teaching and their propositions have had no weight with legislators, for these latter had not been convinced, as only the criminal sociologist could convince them, that punishments are far from having the deterrent force commonly attributed to them, and that crime is not the outcome of free will, but rather a natural phenomenon which can only disappear or diminish when its natural factors are eliminated.

The legislators for their part have not only neglected the definite teaching of these authors with more than ordinary insight, but they have also enacted what are really penal substitutes in a clumsy and unscientific manner.

We have thus studied the data of criminal statistics in their theoretical and practical relations with criminal sociology, and come to the conclusion that, since crime is a natural phenomenon, determined by factors of three kinds, it answers on that account to a law of criminal saturation, whereby the physical and social environment, aided by individual tendencies, hereditary or acquired, and by occasional impulses, necessarily determine the extent of crime in every age and country, both in quantity and quality. That is to say, the criminality of a nation is influenced in the natural sphere by the bio-psychical conditions of individuals and their physical environment, and, in the social sphere, by economic, political, administrative and civil conditions of laws, far more than by the penal code.

Nevertheless the execution of punishment, though it is the less important part of the function of social defence, which should be carried out in harmony with the other functions of society, is always the last and inevitable auxiliary.

And this entirely agrees with the universal law of evolution, in virtue of which, amidst the variation of animal and social organisms, antecedent forms are not wholly eliminated, but continue as the basis of the forms which succeed them. So that if the future evolution of the social administration of defence against crime is to consist in the development of the primitive forms of direct physical coercion into the higher forms of indirect psychical discipline of human activity, this will not imply that the primitive forms must entirely disappear, especially for the gravest crimes, which, in the biological and psychological conditions of those who commit them, take us back to the primitive epochs and forms of individual and social violence.

I end with a modification of an old comparison which has been much abused. Crime has been compared to an impetuous torrent which ought to be enclosed between the dykes of punishment, lest civilised society should be submerged. I do not deny that punishments are the dykes of crime, but I assert that they are dykes of no great strength or utility. All nations know by sad and chronic experience that their dykes cannot save them from inundations; and so our statistics teach us that punishments have but an infinitesimal power against the force of criminality, when its germs are fully developed.

But as we can best protect ourselves against inundations by obeying the laws of hydrostatics and hydrodynamics, by timbering the banks near the source of the stream, and by due rectilineation or excavation along its course and near its mouth, so, in order to defend ourselves against crimes, it is best to observe the laws of psychology and sociology, and to avail ourselves of social substitutes, which are far more efficacious than whole arsenals of repressive measures.

CHAPTER III.

PRACTICAL REFORMS.

The data of criminal anthropology and statistics, and the positive theory of responsibility which flows from them, although they have been systematised only by the positive school, are nevertheless too constantly in evidence not to have made their way into courts and parliaments.

I have already spoken of penal jurisprudence in its relations with criminal sociology, and may now cite a few examples of the more or less direct and avowed influence of the new data on penal legislation.

The legislators of to-day, vaguely impressed by statistical and biological, ethnographical and anthropological data, and still imbued with the old prejudice of social and political artificiality, were at first hurried into a regular mania for legislation, under which every newly observed social phenomenon seemed to demand a special law, regulation, or article in the penal code. Then, as Spencer has said in one of his most brilliant essays, the citizen finds himself in an inextricable network of laws, decrees, regulations and codes, which surround him, support him, fetter and bind him, even before his birth and after his death. For those whom M. Bordier calls the gardeners and trussmakers of society, forgetting the natural character of social phenomena, picture society as so much paste, to which the cook may give any form he pleases, whether pie-crust, dumpling, or tart.

Hence we see on all sides, side by side with dogma in the classical sciences of law, economy, and politics, empiricism in the laws themselves. And that is why the practical defects and constant impotence of repression in penal justice are the most eloquent arguments of the experimental school, which extends and strengthens its own theoretical inductions by the practical reforms which it suggests.

A first example of the influence more directly exercised by the new ideas in penal legislation is furnished by the proposal already realised in the penal laws of Holland, Italy, &c., of two parallel systems of punishment by detention--one for the graver and more dangerous crimes, and the other, ``simple detention," or custodia honesta (``as a first-class misdemeanant"), for contraventions, involuntary offences, and crimes not inspired by the baser passions.

Similarly, the enumeration contained in certain codes, as in Spain, and in the old Mancini draft of a penal code in Italy, of the main aggravating and extenuating circumstances common to all crimes and offences, such as the antecedents of the accused, venial or inexcusable passion, repentance and confession of a crime, extent of injury or the like, is only an elementary and empiric form of the biological and psychological classification of criminals.

Thus also the foundation of asylums for the detention of lunatic criminals, in spite of their being acquitted of moral responsibility; the more and more vigorous, but often too empirical measures against the progressive increase of recidivism; the proposed repressive measures as alternatives to short terms of detention; the reaction against the exaggerations of cellular confinement, which I regard as one of the aberrations of the nineteenth century, are all manifest proofs of the more or less avowed and logical influence of the data of criminal biology and sociology on contemporary penal legislation.

These practical reforms, which, when grafted on the old trunk of the classical theories of crime and punishment, are mere arbitrary and misplaced expedients, really represent, when they are logically co-ordinated and completed, the new system of social defence against crime, which is based on the scientific data and inductions of the positive school, and which it is therefore necessary for us to trace out from its foundations.

I.

In the first place, whilst the positive theories largely reduce the practical importance of the penal code, yet they do more to increase the importance of the rules of penal procedure, which are intended to give practical and daily effect to penal measures, for the defence of society against criminals. For, as I maintained in the Italian Parliament, if the penal code is a code for evil- doers, that of penal procedure is a code for honest people, who are placed on their trial but not yet found guilty.

This is all the more true because, if it is possible to have penal codes whose machinery of psychological coercion is planted on a platonic platform of penitentiary systems written out fair in their symmetrical clauses, but still non-existent, as is the case in Italy, this is not possible in regard to penal procedure. The regulations of the code of ``instruction" must of necessity be carried out by a judicial routine. The penal code may remain a dead letter, as, for instance, when it says that punishment by detention is to be inflicted in prisons constructed with cells; for, happily, the cells necessary in Italy for fifty or sixty thousand prisoners (or in France for thirty or forty thousand) are too expensive to admit of the observance of these articles of the penal code--which nevertheless have cost so many academic discussions as to the best penitentiary system: ``Auburn," ``Philadelphian," ``Irish," or ``progressive." In the organisation of justice, on the other hand, every legal regulation has its immediate application, and therefore reforms of procedure produce immediate and visible results.

It may be added that, if the slight deterrent influence which it is possible for punishment to exercise depends, with its adaptation to various types of criminals, on the certitude and promptitude of its application, the others depend precisely and solely on the organisation of the police, and of penal procedure.

Passing over special and technical reforms which even the classical experts in crime demand in the systems of procedure, and often rather on behalf of the criminals than on behalf of society, we may connect the positive innovations in judicial procedure with these two general principles:--(1) the equal recognition of the rights and guarantees of the prisoner to be tried and of the society which tries him; and (2) the legal sentence, whereof the object is not to define the indeterminable moral culpability of the prisoner, nor the impersonal applicability of an article in the penal code to the crime under consideration; but the application of the law which is most appropriate to the perpetrator of the crime, according to his more or less anti-social characteristics, both physiological and psychological.

From Beccaria onward, penal law developed by reaction against the excessive and arbitrary severity of the Middle Ages--a reaction which led to a progressive decrease of punishments. Similarly official penal procedure in the nineteenth century has been, and continues to be, a reaction against the mediaeval abuses of the inquisitorial system, in the sense of a progressive increase of individual guarantees against the domination of society.

As we considered it necessary in the interests of social self- defence, in the case of criminal law, to combat the individualist excesses of the classical school, so in regard to penal procedure, whilst admitting the irrevocable guarantees of individual liberty, secured under the old system, we think it necessary to restore the equilibrium between individual and social rights, which has been disturbed by the many exaggerations of the classical theories, as we will now proceed to show by a few examples.

The presumption of innocence, and therewith the more general rule, ``in dubio pro reo," is certainly based on an actual truth, and is doubtless obligatory during the progress of the trial. Undetected criminals are fortunately a very small minority as compared with honest people; and we must consequently regard every man who is placed on his trial as innocent until the contrary has been proved.

But when proof to the contrary is evident, as, for instance, in the case of a flagrant crime, or of confession confirmed by other elements in the trial, it seems fit that the presumption should cease in view of absolute fact; and especially when we have to do with habitual criminals.

Even the criminals of this class whom I have questioned recognise a presumption of the opposite kind. ``They have convicted me," said an habitual thief, ``because they knew I might have done it, without any proof; and they were in the right. You will never be convicted, because you never stole; and if we happen to be innocent once in a way, that must be set against the other times when we are not discovered." And the ironical smile of several of these prisoners, condemned on circumstantial evidence, reminded me of a provision which was once proposed in the Italian penal code, under which a person surprised in the attempt to commit a crime, if it was not known what precise form his crime would have taken, was to be found guilty of a less serious offence. This might be good for an occasional criminal, or a criminal of passion, but would be absurd and dangerous for habitual criminals and old offenders.

The exaggerations of the presumption ``in dubio pro reo'' are due to a sort of mummification and degeneracy of the legal maxims, whereby propositions based upon observation and generalisation from existing facts continue in force and are mechanically applied after the facts have changed or ceased to exist.

What reason can there be for extending provisional freedom, pending an appeal, to one who has already been found guilty and liable to punishment for a crime or offence, under sentence of a court of first instance? To presume the innocence of every one during the first trial is reasonable; but to persist in a presumption which has been destroyed by facts, after a first condemnation, would be incomprehensible if it were not a manifestly exaggerated outcome of classical and individualist theories, which can only see a ``victim of authority'' in every accused person, and in every condemned person also.

Another point is that of acquittal in case of an equality of votes, especially where born and habitual criminals are concerned. I think it would be much more reasonable to restore the verdict of ``not proven,'' which the Romans admitted under the form of ``non liquet,'' as an alternative to ``absolvo'' and ``condemno,'' and which may be delivered by juries in Scotland. Every one who has been put on his trial is entitled to have his innocence declared, if it has been actually proved. But if the proofs remain incomplete, his only right is not to be condemned, since his culpability has not been proved. But it is not the duty of society to declare him absolutely innocent, when suspicious circumstances remain. In this case the only logical and just verdict is one of ``not proven.'' Such a verdict would obliterate the shadow of doubt which rests on persons who have been acquitted, by reason of the identical verdicts in cases of proved innocence and inadequacy of proof, and on the other hand it would avoid the tendency to compromise, under which judges and juries, in place of acquitting when the proof is insufficient, sometimes prefer to convict, but make the punishment lighter.

Another case of exaggeration in the presumption of innocence is afforded by the regulations as to contradictory or irregular verdicts, which may be corrected only when there has been a conviction; whilst if the error has led to the acquittal of an accused person, it cannot be put right. The influence of the individualist and classical school is here manifest, for, as M. Majno says, ``the justice of sentences rests as much on just condemnations as upon just acquittals." If the individual has a right to claim that he shall not be condemned through the mistake or ignorance of his judges, society also has the right to demand that those whose acquittal is equally the result of mistake or ignorance shall not be allowed to go free.

On the same ground of equilibrium between the rights of the individual and the rights of society, which the positive school aims at restoring, something must be said as to the regulation by which, if the appeal is brought by a condemned person, the punishment cannot be increased. One classical expert in an official position would not even give the right to appeal at all.

Now if appeal is allowed for the purpose of correcting possible mistakes on the part of the original judges, why must we allow this correction in mitigation, and not in increase of punishment? And to this practical assurance of the condemned person that he has nothing to fear from a second trial, which seems to have been given to him for the sole purpose of encouraging him to abuse his power, since appeals are too often a mere dilatory pretext, there is a pendant in the right of the public prosecutor to demand a re- hearing, but only ``in the interest of the law, and without prejudice to the person acquitted."

A last instance of the same kind of protective regulation for the protection of evil-doers is to be found in the new trials which are permitted only in cases where there has been a condemnation, and that on arbitrary and superficial grounds. Most of the classical commentators on procedure do not dream of the possibility of revision in the case of acquittals, and yet, as Majno justly says, ``even if he has profited by false witness, forged documents, intimidation or corruption of a judge, or any other offence, the acquitted person calmly enjoys his boast, and can even plume himself on his own share in the business without fear of being put on his trial again." The Austrian and German codes of procedure admit revision in cases of acquittal; and the positive rule in this connection ought to be that a case should be re-heard when the sentence of condemnation or acquittal is evidently erroneous.

From the same principle of equality between the guarantees of the individual criminal and of honest society we infer the necessity of greater strictness in the indemnification of the victims of crime. For the platonic damages now added to all sorts of sentences, but nearly always ineffectual, we believe that a strict obligation ought to be substituted, the operation of which should be superintended by the State, in the same way as the other consequence of the crime, which is called the punishment. I will return to this when I trace the outline of the positive system of social defence against criminals.

The positive school, precisely because it aims at an equilibrium between individual and social rights, is not content with taking the part of society against the individual. It also takes the part of the individual against society.

In the first place, the very reforms which we propose for the indemnification of the victims of crime, regarded as a social function, as well as the operation of the punishment, have an individualist character. The individualism of the classical school was not even complete as a matter of fact: for the guarantees which it proposed took account of the individual criminal only, and did not touch his victims, who are also individuals, and far more worthy of sympathy and protection.

But, beyond this, we may point to three reforms as an instance of the positive and reasonable guarantees of the individual against the abuse or the defects of social authority. Of these reforms two have been put forward by the classical school also, but, like criminal lunatic asylums, alternatives for short terms of imprisonment, and so on, they have generally remained inoperative, for they are not in harmony with the bulk of traditional theory, and only in a positive system have they any organic and efficacious connection with the data of criminal sociology. I refer to the exercise of popular opinion, the correction of judicial mistakes, and the transfer of sundry punishable offences to the category of civil contraventions.

The institution of a Ministry of Justice corresponds to the demands of general sociology, which exacts division of labour even in collective organisms, and to those of criminal sociology, which requires a special and distinct organ for the social function of defence against crime. Indeed it has become indispensable as a necessary judicial organ, even in nations like England which have not yet formally established it. So that, far from confounding the Public Prosecutor with the judicial body, we see the necessity of giving to this office a more elevated character and a distinct personality, with ampler guarantees of independence of the executive power.

Nevertheless the action of the Ministry of Justice, as now commonly organised, may be inadequate for the protection of the victims of crime, either indirectly through the insufficient number of its functionaries, or directly, through the functional defect insisted on by M. Gneist, ``party spirit or prejudice in favour of the governing powers.'' The latter, indeed, notwithstanding M. Glaser's objection that government pressure is impossible, have no need to give special instructions, of a more or less compromising character, in order to exercise a special influence in any particular case. There is no necessity for anything beyond the conservative spirit natural to every institution of the State, or the principle of authority which is a special form of it, apart from the less respectable motives of interested subservience to such as are in office and dispense promotion.

Hence it will be useful, in initiating criminal proceedings, to add to the action of a Public Prosecutor (but not to substitute for him) the action of private persons.

Criminal proceedings by citizens may take two forms, according as they are put in operation only by the injured person or by any individual.

The first mode, already allowed in every civilised nation, needs amendment in various ways, especially in regard to the subordination of the penal action to the plaint of the injured person, which ought to be restrained, and even abolished. In fact, whereas this right has hitherto been regulated by law only in view of the legal and material gravity of the offence, it should in future be made to depend on the perversity of the offender; for society has a much greater interest in defending itself against the author of a slight offence if he is a born criminal or a criminal lunatic, than in defending itself against the author of a more serious crime, if he is an occasional criminal or a criminal of passion. And the necessity of bringing a private action in regard to certain offences is only a source of abuses, and of demoralising bargains between offenders and injured persons.

On the other hand, this prosecution by a citizen who has been injured by a crime or an offence ought to have more efficacious guarantees, either for the exercise of the rights of the injured person, or against the possible neglect or abuse of the Public Prosecutor. If, indeed, he is obliged to take up every charge and action, he is also (in Italy and France, but not in Austria or Germany, for instance) the only authority as to penal actions, and consequently as to penal judgments.

In Italy, out of 264,038 cases which came before the Public Prosecutor in 1880, six per cent., or 16,058, were ``entered on the records,'' or, in other words, they were not followed up; and in 1889, out of a total of 271,279, the number of unprosecuted cases was 27,086, or ten per cent. That is, the number had almost doubled in ten years.

In France the annual average of plaints, charges, and trials with which the Public Prosecutor was concerned stood at 114,181 in the years 1831-5; at 371,910 in 1876-80; and at 459,319 in 1887. And the cases not proceeded with were 34,643, or thirty per cent., in 1831-5; 181,511, or forty-eight per cent., in 1876-80; and 239,061, or fifty-two per cent., in 1887. That is to say, their actual and relative numbers mere nearly doubled in fifty years.

Is it possible that in ten, or even in fifty years, the moral conditions of a nation, and its inclination to bring criminal charges, should be so modified that the number of cases devoid of foundation should have been almost doubled? It is certain that in different nations and different provinces there are varying degrees of readiness to bring charges against lawbreakers rather than to take personal vengeance. But in one and the same nation this vindictive spirit and this readiness to bring charges cannot vary so greatly and rapidly, especially within ten years, as in Italy; for the persistence of popular sentiment is a well- known fact. It is rather in the disposition of the functionaries of the Ministry of Justice, which is far more variable, that we must look for an explanation of this fact, which is also accounted for by the tendency to diminish the statistical records of crime.

Now, why must the citizen who lodges a complaint of what he considers a crime or offence submit to the decision of the Public Prosecutor, who has allowed his action to drop? This consideration has led to the subsidiary penal action, already allowed in Germany and Austria, and introduced in the draft codes of procedure in Hungary, Belgium, and France, which is a genuine guarantee of the individual as against the social authority. We must not, however, deceive ourselves as to the efficacy or frequency of its operation, especially in the Latin nations, which have none too much individual initiative.

The second form of private prosecution is that of the ``popular punitive action,'' which existed in the Roman penal law--which, it may be said in passing, is not so insignificant as the classical school has supposed. The statement of M. Carrara, too often repeated, that ``The Romans, who were giants in civil law, are pigmies in penal law,'' is not in my opinion correct. It is true that the Roman penal law was not organised in a philosophical system; but it exhibits throughout the wonderfully practical judgment of the Roman jurisconsults; and indeed one cannot see why they should have lost this sense when dealing with crimes and punishments. On the other hand, I am inclined to think that the importance of the Roman civil law has been exaggerated, and that the spirit of the corpus juris springs from social and economic conditions so different from our own that we can no longer feel bound to submit to its tyranny. The penal law of the Romans, however, contains several maxims based on unquestionable common sense, which deserve to be rescued from the oblivion to which they have been condemned by the dogmatism of the classical school. Examples of these are the popular punitive action; the distinction between dolus bonus and dolus malus, which belongs to the theory of motives; the stress laid upon intentions rather than upon their actual outcome; the law of exceptio veritatis in cases of slander, which under the pharisaism of the classical theory serves only to give immunity to knaves; the penalty of twofold or threefold restitution for theft, in place of a few days or weeks in prison; the condemnation of the most hardened criminals to the mines, instead of providing them with cells, as comfortable as they are ineffectual--apart from the consideration that the firedamp in mines and the unhealthiness of penal settlements would be less mischievous if their victims were the most dangerous criminals rather than honest miners and husbandmen.

To return to the popular penal action, it is so commonly advocated, even by the classical school, that it is necessary to say another word on the subject.

Gneist, from his special point of view, proposed that this action should be introduced into penal procedure, as against electoral and press offences, offences against the law of public meetings and associations, and the abuse of public authority. But I consider that this action would be a necessary guarantee, in the case of all crimes and offences, for a reasonable and definite adjustment of the rights of the individual and of society.

Another reform, tending to a more effective guarantee of individual rights, is the revision of judicial errors in the interests of all who are unjustly condemned or prosecuted. Such a reform has been advocated also by several members of the classical school; but it seemed only too likely to remain with them a mere benevolent expression of opinion; for it can only be carried into effect by curtailing imprisonment, and by a more frequent and stringent infliction of fines, as advocated by the positive school.

Sanctioned in some special cases, as an exceptional measure--as, for instance, in the last century by the Parliament of Toulouse, and in our age by the English Parliament--compensation for judicial errors was rendered necessary in France at the end of the eighteenth century, after a series of unjust condemnations, even death sentences, which led Voltaire and Beccaria to demand the abolition of capital punishment. In 1781 the Society of Art and Literature at Chalonssur-Marne offered a prize for an essay on the subject, and awarded it to Brissot de Warville, for his work, ``Le Sang Innocent Venge.'' In the records of the Etats Generaux there were many votes in favour of this reform, which Louis XVI. caused to be introduced on May 8, 1788. In 1790 Duport brought in a measure in the Constituent Assembly; but it was rejected after a short discussion in February, 1791, during which the same practical objections were urged as have been repeated up to the present time. Nevertheless, the Convention decreed special indemnities, as, for instance. a thousand francs in 1793 for one Busset, ``for arbitrary imprisonment and prosecution.'' In 1823 the above-named Society at Chalonssur- Marne proposed the same subject for an essay; and it has been the object of sundry proposals, all rejected, as in 1867 during the discussion on criminal appeals, on amendments moved by Jules Favre, Richard, and Ollivier; and again in 1883 by Depute Pieyre, and in 1890 by Depute Reinach.

This reform has been advocated by Necker, amongst other writers, in his memoir on ``Financial Administration in France,'' and by Pastoret, Voltaire, Bentham, Merlin, Legraverend, Helie, Tissot, and more comprehensively by Marsangy in his ``Reform of the Criminal Law'' (1864). Marsangy advocated many other practical reforms which have since been adopted, in substitution for the objectionable short terms of imprisonment. More recently the subject has been treated in France by the magistrates Bernard, Pascaud, Nicolas, Giacobbi, and by the Attorney-Generals Molines, Jourdan, Houssard, Dupry, Bujard, in their inaugural addresses.

In Italy there was a notable precedent for this reform in the Treasury of Fines, established for Tuscany in 1786, and for the kingdom of the Two Sicilies in the penal code of 1819, for the purpose of creating a fund for compensation in cases of judicial error. In 1886 Deputy Pavesi brought in a measure which was not discussed; and this indemnification, which had already been proposed in 1873 by De Falco, keeper of the seals, in his draft of an Italian penal code, was not included in subsequent Bills, mainly on account of the financial difficulties. Amongst writers on criminology, it was advocated in Italy by Carrara, Pessina, and Brusa; in Germany by Geyer and Schwarze; in Belgium by Prins and others, and more recently by M. Garofalo, in his report to the third National Congress on Law, at Florence, in September, 1891.

Amongst existing laws, indemnification for judicial errors, whether limited to cases in which the innocence of condemned persons can be proved, or extended to persons wrongfully prosecuted, is included in the penal codes of Hungary and Mexico, and by special laws in Portugal (1884), Sweden (1886), Denmark (1888), and especially in Switzerland, in the cantons of Fribourg, Vaud, Neuchatel, Geneva, Bale, and Berne.

The legal principle that the State ought to indemnify material and moral injury inflicted by its functionaries, through malice or negligence, on a citizen who has done nothing to subject himself to prosecution or condemnation, cannot be seriously contested. But the whole difficulty is reduced to deciding in what cases the right to indemnification ought to be recognised, and then to providing a fund out of which the State can discharge this duty.

For the latter purpose it would be necessary to include an adequate sum in the Budget. This was done in Bavaria, in 1888, by setting apart 5,000 marks annually; and the first who profited by this provision received a pension of 300 marks per annum, after being rendered incapable of work by seven years' imprisonment for a crime which he had not committed. But if the policy of retrenchment imposed on the European States by their insane military expenditure and their chronic wars prevents the carrying out of this proposal, there is the Italian precedent of the Treasury of Fines, which, with the fines inflicted, or which ought to be inflicted on convicted persons, and the product of prison labour, would provide the necessary amount for the indemnities which the State ought to pay to innocent persons who have been condemned or prosecuted, as well as to the victims of offences.

As for the cases in which a right to indemnification for judicial errors ought to be acknowledged, it seems to me evident in the first place that we must include those of convicted persons found to be innocent on a revision of the sentence. Amongst persons wrongfully prosecuted, I think an indemnity is due to those who have been acquitted because their action was neither a crime nor an offence, or because they had no part in the action (whence also follows the necessity of verdicts of Not Proven, so as to distinguish cases of acquittal on the ground of proved innocence)-- always provided that the prosecuted persons have not given a reasonable pretext for their trial by their own conduct, or their previous relapse, or their habitual criminality.

The third proposition of the positive school in regard to individual guarantees, which was also advanced by M. Puglia, is connected with reform of the penal code, and especially with the more effectual indemnification of the victims of crime. The object is to prune the long and constantly increasing list of crimes, offences, and contraventions of all acts which result in slight injury, committed by occasional offenders, or ``pseudo- criminals"--that is, by normal persons acting merely with negligence or imprudence.

In these cases the personal and social injury is not caused maliciously, and the agent is not dangerous, so that imprisonment is more than ever inappropriate, unjust, and even dangerous in its consequences. Deeds of this kind ought to be eliminated from the penal code, and to be regarded merely as civil offences, as SIMPLE theft was by the Romans; for a strict indemnification will be for the authors of these deeds a more effectual and at the same time a less demoralising and dangerous vindication of the law than the grotesque condemnation to a few days or weeks in prison.

It will be understood that the classical theory of absolute and eternal justice cannot concern itself with these trifles, which, nevertheless, constitute two-thirds of our daily social and judicial existence; for, according to this theory, there is always an offence to be visited with a proportionate punishment, just as with a murder, or a highway robbery, or a slanderous word. But for the positive school, which realises the actual and practical conditions of social and punitive justice, there is on the other hand an evident need of relieving the codes, tribunals, and prisons from these microbes of the criminal world, by excluding all punishments by imprisonment for what Venturi and Turati happily describe as the atomic particles of crime, and by relaxing in some degree that monstrous network of prohibitions and punishments which is so inflexible for petty transgressors and offenders, but so elastic for serious evil-doers.

II.

The reforms which we propose in punitive law are based on the fundamental principle already established on the data of anthropology and criminal statistics.

If the ethical idea of punishment as a retribution for crime be excluded from the repressive function of society, and if we regard this function simply as a defensive power acting through law, penal justice can no longer be squared with a minute computation of the moral responsibility or culpability of the criminal. It can have no other end than to prove, first, that the person under trial is the author of the crime, and, then, to which type of criminals he belongs, and, as a consequence, what degree of anti-social depravity and re-adaptability is indicated by his physical and mental qualities.

The first and fundamental inquiry in every criminal trial will always be the verification of the crime and the identification of the criminal.

But when the connection of the accused and the crime is once established, either the accused produces evidence of his honesty, or of the uprightness of his motives-- the only case in which his acquittal can be demanded or taken into consideration--or else it is proved that his motives were anti-social and unlawful, and then there is no place for those grotesque and often insincere contests between the prosecution and the defence to prevent or to secure an acquittal, which will be impossible whatever may be the psychological conditions of the criminal. The one and only possible issue between the prosecution and the defence will be to determine, by the character--of the accused and of his action, to what anthropological class he belongs, whether he is a born criminal, or mad, or an habitual or occasional criminal, or a criminal of passion.

In this case we shall have no more of those combats of craft, manipulations, declamations, and legal devices, which make every criminal trial a game of chance, destroying public confidence in the administration of justice, a sort of spider's web which catches flies and lets the wasps escape.

The crime will always be the object of punitive law, even under the positive system of procedure; but, instead of being the exclusive concern of the judge it will only be the ground of procedure, and one symptom amongst others of the depravation and re-adaptability of the criminal, who will himself be the true and living subject of the trial. As it is, the whole trial is developed from the material fact; and the whole concern of the judge is to give it a legal definition, so that the criminal is always in the background, regarded merely as the ultimate billet for a legal decision, in accordance with some particular article in the penal code--except that the actual observance of this article is at the mercy of a thousand accidents of which the judge knows nothing, and which are all foreign to the crime, and to the criminal.

If we rid ourselves of the assumption that we can measure the moral culpability of the accused, the whole process of a criminal trial consists in the assemblage of facts, the discussion, and the decision upon the evidence. For the classical school, on the other hand, such a trial has been regarded as a succession of guarantees for the individual against society, and, by a sort of reaction against the methods of legal proof, has been made to turn upon the private conviction, not to say the intuition, of the judge and counsel.

A criminal trial ought to retrace the path of the crime itself, passing backward from the criminal action (a violation of the law), in order to discover the criminal, and, in the psychological domain, to establish the determining motives and the anthropological type. Hence arises the necessity for the positive school of reconsidering the testimony in a criminal case, so as to give it its full importance, and to reinforce it with the data and inferences not only of ordinary psychology, as the classical school has always done (Pagano for instance, and Bentham, Mittermaier, Ellero, and others), but also, and above all, with the data and inferences of criminal anthropology and psychology.

In the evolution of the theory of evidence we may distinguish four characteristic stages, as M. Tarde observed--the religious stage, with its ordeals and combats; the legal stage, accompanied by torture; the political stage, with private conviction and the jury; and the scientific stage, with expert knowledge of experimental results, systematically collected and studied, which is the new task of positive procedure.

We must glance at each of the three elements of the criminal trial: collection of evidence (police and preliminary inquiry); discussion of evidence (prosecution and defence), and decision upon evidence (judges and juries).

It is evident in the first place, as I remarked in the first edition of this work, and as Righini, Garofalo, Lombroso, Alongi, and Rossi have confirmed, that a study of the anthropological factors of crime provides the guardians and administrators of the law with new and more certain methods in the detection of the guilty. Tattooing, anthropometry, physiognomy, physical and mental conditions, records of sensibility, reflex activity, vaso- motor reactions, the range of sight, the data of criminal statistics, facilitate and complete the amassing of evidence, personal identification, and hints as to the capacity to commit any particular crime; and they will frequently suffice to give police agents and examining magistrates a scientific guidance in their inquiries, which now depend entirely on their individual acuteness and mental sagacity.

And when we remember the enormous number of crimes and offences which are not punished, for lack or inadequacy of evidence, and the frequency of trials which are based solely on circumstantial hints, it is easy to see the practical utility of the primary connection between criminal sociology and penal procedure.

The practical application of anthropometry to the identification of criminals, and to the question of recidivism, which was begun in Paris by M. Bertillon, and subsequently adopted by almost all the states of Europe and America, is too familiar to need description. It will be sufficient to recall the modifications of Bertillon's system by Anfosso, with the actual collection of anthropometric data, and their inclusion in the ordinary records of justice.

Thus the sphygmographic data on the circulation of the blood, which reveal the inner emotions, in spite of an outward appearance of calm or indifference, have already served to show that a person accused of theft was not guilty of it, but that he was on the contrary guilty of another theft, of which he had not been so much as suspected. On another occasion they established the innocence of a man condemned to death. We shall have more speaking and frequent illustrations when these inquiries have been placed regularly at the service of criminal justice.

The sphygmograph may also be useful in the diagnosis of simulated disease, after the example set M. Voisin in the case of a sham epileptic in Paris, ``whose sphygmographic lines have no resemblance to those of true epileptics before and after a fit, and only resemble those produced by normal persons after a violent gesticulation "

As for the possible utilisation of hypnotism, we must be cautious before we draw any legal conclusions from it; but it cannot be questioned that this is a valuable source of scientific aid in the systematic collection of criminal evidence.

But, for the present, the most certain and profitable aids in the collection of evidence are those afforded by the organic and psychical characteristics of criminals. In my study on homicide I reckoned up many psychological and psycho-pathological symptoms which characterise the murderer, the homicidal madman, and the homicide through passion. And in my professional practice I have often found by experience that there is a great suggestive efficacy in these psychological symptoms in regard to the conduct of a criminal, before, during, and after a crime; and it is important to bring this knowledge scientifically before detectives and judges.

These data are not applicable to accused persons exclusively. When we remember the enormous importance of oral evidence in the chain of criminal proof, and the rough traditional empiricism of the criteria of credibility, which are daily applied in all trials to all kinds of witnesses, by men who regard them, like the prisoners, as an average abstract type--excluding only the definite cases of inability to give evidence, which are defined beforehand with as much method as the cases of irresponsibility-- the necessity of calling in the aid of scientific psychology and psycho-pathology is manifest.

For instance, not to dwell on the absurd violation of these traditional criteria of credibility, when police officers are admitted as witnesses (often the only witnesses) of resistance to authority or violence, wherein they are doubly interested parties, how often in our courts do we give a thought to the casual imaginations or credulity of children, women, weak-nerved or hysterical persons, and so on? Counsel for defence or prosecution who desired to know if any particular witness is or is not hysterical would bring a smile to the face of the judge, very learned, no doubt, in Roman law or legal precedents, but certainly ignorant in physiology, psychology, and psycho-pathology. Yet the tendency to slander in hysterical cases, which M. Ceneri urged so eloquently in a celebrated trial or the tendency to untruth in children, which M. Motet has ably illustrated, are but manifest and simple examples of this applicability of normal, criminal, and pathological psychology to the credibility of witnesses. And, under its influence, how much of the clear atmosphere of humanity will stimulate our courts of justice, which are still too much isolated from the world and from human life, where, nevertheless, prisoners and witnesses come, and too often come again, living phantoms whom the judges know not, and only see confusedly through the thick mist of legal maxims, and articles of the code, and criminal procedure.

Apart from these examples, which prove the importance of what M. Sarraute justly called ``judicial applications of criminal sociology,'' the fundamental reform needed in the scientific preparation of criminal evidence is the creation of magisterial experts in every court of preliminary inquiry. In a question of forgery, poisoning, or abortion, the judge has recourse to experts in handwriting, chemistry, or obstetrics; but beyond these technical, special, and less frequent cases, in every criminal trial the basis of inquiry is or ought to be formed by the data of criminal biology, psychology, and psycho-pathology. So that, over and above the knowledge of these sciences which is necessary to judges, magistrates, and police officers, it is most important that an expert, or several experts in criminal anthropology should be attached to every court of criminal inquiry.

This would provide us with an anthropological classification, certain and speedy, of every convicted person, as well as a legal classification of the material fact, and we should avoid the scandal of what are known as experts for the prosecution and experts for the defence. There should be but one finding of experts, either by agreement between them or by a scientific reference to arbitration, as in the German, Austrian, and Russian system; and over this finding the judges and the litigants should have no other power than to call for explanations from the chief of the experts.

In this way we should further avoid the scandal of judges entirely ignorant of the elementary ideas of criminal biology, psychology, and psycho-pathology, like the president of an assize court whom I heard telling a jury that he was unable to say why an expert ``wanted to examine the feet of a prisoner in order to come to a decision about his head.'' This president, who was an excellent magistrate and a learned jurist was wholly unacquainted with the elements of the theory of degeneracy, like one of his colleagues whom I heard saying, when the expert spoke of the abnormal shape of the ears of a prisoner (in accord with the inquiries of Morel and Lombroso), ``That depends on how the hat is worn.''

For in consequence of the assumption, made by Kant amongst others, that questions of mental disease belong to the philosopher rather than to the physician, and of the absurd and shallow idea which superficial persons entertain of those who are insane, picturing them as constantly raving, the judge or juryman who pins his faith to an expert in handwriting thinks himself above the necessity of taking the opinion of an expert in insanity.

It must be recognised, however, that this foolish assumption is partly due to a reasonable anxiety for the public safety, under the sway of the classical theories, which allow the acquittal and discharge of criminals who are found to be of unsound mind. It will eventually disappear, either by the wider diffusion of elementary ideas of psycho-pathology or by the application of positive theories, which are far from carrying the proved insanity of a prisoner to the dangerous and absurd conclusion of his acquittal.

After the first stage of the collection of evidence, during which we can admit the legal representation of the accused, especially for the sake of eliciting both sides of the question, without, however, going so far as the individual exaggerations of complete publicity for the preliminary inquiry, we come to the second stage of procedure, that of the public discussion of the evidence.

The principals in this discussion represent the prosecution (public or private) and the defence; and for these, as I cannot go into great detail, I will only mention one necessary reform. That is the institution of a sort of public defence, by a legal officer such as used to be found in certain of the Italian provinces, under the title of ``advocate of the poor,'' who ought to be on a par with the public prosecutor, and to be substituted for the present institution of the official defence, which is a complete failure.

As for the actual discussion of evidence, when we have established the scientific rules of evidence, based upon expert acquaintance with criminal anthropology, and when we have eliminated all verbal contention over the precise measure of moral responsibility in the prisoner, the whole debate will be a criticism of the personal and material indications, of the determining motives, and the anthropological category to which the accused belongs, and of the consequent form of social defence best adapted to his physical and psychical character.

The practical conclusion of the criminal trial is arrived at in the third stage, that of the decision on the evidence.

So far as we are concerned, the criminal adjudication has the simple quality of a scientific inquiry, subjective and objective, in regard to the accused as a possible criminal, and in relation to the deed of which he is alleged to be the author. We naturally therefore require in the judge certain scientific knowledge, and not merely the intuition of common sense.

But as the consultation of the jury, by reason of its inseparable political aspect, must take place in private, we can only insist on the fundamental reform of the judicial organisation, which alone can realise the scientific principle of criminal adjudication. It was Garofalo who, in the earlier days of the positive school, urged that civil and criminal judges ought to be wholly distinct, and that the latter ought to be versed in anthropology, statistics, and criminal sociology, rather than in Roman law, legal history, and the like, which throw no light on the judgment of the criminal.

Learned jurists, proficient in the civil law, are least fit to make a criminal judge, accustomed as they are by their studies to abstractions of humanity, looking solely to the juridical bearings, inasmuch as civil law is mostly ignorant of all that concerns the physical and moral nature of individuals. The demoralisation or uprightness of a creditor, for instance, has no influence for or against the validity of his credit.

The jurist, therefore, in a matter of criminal adjudication, entirely loses sight of the personal conditions of the accused, and the social conditions of the community, and confines his attention to the deed, and to the maxims of a so-called retributive justice. They who are called upon to try criminals ought to possess the ideas necessary to the natural study of a criminal man, and should therefore constitute an order of magistrates wholly distinct from that of civil judges.

The practical means of securing this fundamental reform of the judicial bench ought to begin with the organisation of the university, for in the courses of the faculty of law it will be necessary to introduce a more vigorous and modern stream of social and anthropological studies, which must also eventually put new life into the ancient maxims of the civil law.

In the second place, law students at the university ought to be admitted to what Ellero called a science of clinical criminology, that is to interviews with and systematic observations of prisoners. The first Congress of Criminal Anthropology approved the proposal of M. Tarde, upon the following motion of Moleschot- Ferri:-- ``The Congress, in agreement with the scientific tendency of criminal anthropology, is of opinion that prison authorities, whilst taking necessary precautions for internal discipline, and for the individual rights of condemned prisoners, should admit to the clinical study of criminals all professors and students of penal law and legal medicine, under the direction and responsibility of their own professors, and if possible in the character of societies for the aid of actual and discharged prisoners."

Lastly, a special school should be founded for policemen and prison warders, with the object of securing detectives distinguished not only for their personal ability, but also for their knowledge of criminal biology and psychology.

To these reforms, which guarantee the scientific capacity of the criminal judge, we must add reforms which would secure his complete independence of the executive authority, which is now the only authority responsible for the advancement and allocation of judges. But this independence would not be exempt from every kind of control, such as public opinion, and disciplinary authority to some extent distinct from the personnel of the bench; for otherwise the judicial authority would soon become another form of insupportable tyranny.

The most effectual mode of securing the independence of the judges is to improve their position in life. For admitting that a fixed stipend, payable every month, makes a man content with a somewhat lower figure, still it is certain that in these days, with a few honourable exceptions, the selection of judges is not satisfactory, because low salaries only attract such as could not earn more by the practice of their profession.

The personal character of the bench vitally affects the quality of the government as a whole. The most academic and exalted codes are of little avail if there are not good judges to administer them; but with good judges it matters little if the codes or statutes are imperfect.

In criminal law the application of the statute to the particular case is not, or should not be, a mere question of legal and abstract logic, as it is in civil law. It involves the adaptation of an abstract rule, in a psychological sense, to a living and breathing man; for the criminal judge cannot separate himself from the environment and social life, so as to become a more or less mechanical lex loquens. The living and human tests of every criminal sentence reside in the conditions of the act, the author, and reacting society, far more than in the written law.

Herein we have an opportunity of solving the old question of the authority of the judge, wherein we have gone from one excess to another, from the unbounded authority of the Middle Ages to the Baconian aphorism respecting the law and the judge, according to which the law is excellent when it leaves least to the judge, and the judge is excellent when he leaves himself the least independent judgment.

If the function of the criminal judge were always to be, as it is now, an illusory and quantitative inquiry into the moral culpability of the accused, with the equally quantitative and Byzantine rules on attempt, complicity, competing crimes, and so forth--that is to say, if the law were to be applied to the crime and not to the criminal, then it is necessary that the authority of the judge should be restrained within the numerical barriers of articles of the code, of so many years, months, and days of imprisonment to be dosed out, just as the Chinese law decides with much exactitude the length and diameter of the bamboo rods, which in the penal system of the Celestial Empire have the same prominence as penitentiary cells have with us.

But if a criminal trial ought to be, on the other hand, a physio- psychological examination of the accused, the crime being relegated to the second line, as far as punishment is concerned, the criminal being kept in the front, then it is clear that the penal code should be limited to a few general rules on the modes of defence and social sanction, and on the constituent elements of every crime and offence, whilst the judge should have greater liberty, controlled by the scientific and positive data of the trial, so that he may judge the man before him with a knowledge of humanity.

The unfettered authority of the judge is inadmissible in regard to the forms of procedure, which for the prosecuted citizen are an actual guarantee against judicial errors and surprises, but which should be carefully distinguished from that hollow and superstitious formalism which generates the most grotesque inanities, such as an error of a word in the oath taken by witnesses or experts, or a blot of ink on the signature of a clerk.

III.

Scientific knowledge of criminals and of crime, not only as the deed which preceded the trial, but also as a natural and social phenomenon--this, then, is the fundamental principle of every reform in the judicial order; and this, too, is a condemnation of the jury. Whilst Brusa, one of the most doctrinaire of the Italian classical school, foretold a steady decline of the ``technical element'' in the magistracy, and consequently a persistent intervention of the popular influence in the administration of justice, the positive school, on the other hand, has always predicted the inevitable decline of the jury in the trial of crimes and ordinary offences.[16]

[16] It is interesting to observe that Carrara, in spite of

his public advocacy of the jury, wrote in a private letter in 1870 (published on the unveiling of his monument at Lucca):--``I expressed my opinion as to the jury in 1841, in an article published in the Annals of Tuscan Jurisprudence--namely, that criminal justice was becoming a lottery. Justice is being deprived of her scales and provided with a dice-box. This seems to me to be the capital defect of the jury. All other defects might be eliminated by a good law, but this one is inseparable from the jury. . . . Even amongst magistrates we may find the harsh and the clement; but in the main they judge according to legal argument, and one can always more or less foresee the issue of a trial. But with juries all forecast is rash and deceptive. They decide by sentiment; and what is there more vague and fickle than sentiment. . . . With juries, craft is more serviceable to an advocate than knowledge. I once had to defend a husband who had killed his wife's lover in a cafe. I challenged the bachelors on the jury, and accepted the married men. After that, I was sure of success, and I succeeded. . . . This is the real essential vice of the jury, which no legislative measure could overcome.''

Theodore Jouffroy, after listening at the University of Pisa to a lecture by Carmignani against the jury, said, ``You are defending logic, but slaying liberty.''

Apart from the question whether liberty is possible without logic, it is nevertheless a fact that there is always a prominent political character in the jury. This accounts for the more or less declamatory defences of this judicial institution, which is no favourite with the criminal sociologist.

At the end of the eighteenth century, when there was a scientific and legislative tendency towards the creation of an independent order of magistrates, the French Revolution, mistrusting the whole aristocracy and social caste, opposed this tendency, believing enthusiastically in the omnipotence and omniscience of the people, and instituted the jury. And whilst in the political order it was inspired by classical antiquity, in the order of justice it adopted this institution from England. The jury was not unknown to the Republic of Athens and Rome, but it was developed in the Middle Ages by the ``barbarians,'' as an instrument which helped the people to escape from tyranny in the administration of the law. It used to be said that the jury made a reality of popular sovereignty, and substituted the common sense and good will of the people for the cold dogmatism of the lawyers, penetrated as they were by class prejudices. From this point of view the jury was too much in accord with the general tendency of the ideas of the day not to be greedily adopted. It was another example of the close connection between philosophic ideas, political institutions, and the judicial organisation.

The jury, transported to the Continent, in spite of the improvements recorded by Bergasse in his report to the Constituent Assembly, on August 14, 1789, was a mere counterfeit of that which it was, and is, in England. But its political character is still so attractive that it has many supporters to this day, though the results of its employment in various countries are not very happy.

Yet, as the jury is a legal institution, we must consider its advantages and defects, both from the political and from the legal point of view, and accept the conclusion forced upon us by the predominance of one or the other.

From the political standpoint, it is unquestionable that the jury is a concession to popular sovereignty; for it is admitted that the power of the law not only originates with the people, but is also directly exercised by them.

The jury may also be a guarantee of civic and political liberties as against the abuses of government, which are far more easy with a small number of judges, more or less subordinate to the government.

Again, the jury may be a means of affirming the sentiment of equality amongst citizens, each of whom may to-morrow become a judge of his equals, and of spreading political education, with a practical knowledge of the law. It is true that, with this knowledge of the law, juries also learn the details of every kind of crime, without the equally constant evidence of virtuous actions; and there is here a danger of moral contagion from crime. But, from the political point of view, it is certain that the jury may awaken, with a knowledge of the law, a consciousness of civic duties, which are too frequently undertaken as a forced and troublesome burden.

On these political advantages of the jury, however, a few remarks may be made.

101

In the first place, the concession to popular sovereignty is reduced to very small proportions by the limitations of the jury list, and of the functions of the jury, which legislation in every country is compelled to impose.

The essential characteristic distinguishing the jury from the judge is especially marked by the origin of their authority; for the jury is a judge simply because he is a citizen, whilst the magistrate is a judge only by popular election or appointment by the head of the State. So that any one who has entered on his civil and political rights, and is of the necessary age, ought, according to the spirit of the institution, to administer justice on every civil or criminal question, whatever its importance, and not only in giving the final verdict, but also in conducting the trial. Yet not only is the ancient trial by popular assemblies impossible in the great States of our day, but also faith in the omniscience of the people has not availed to prevent all kinds of limitations in the principle of the jury. Thus the political principle of the jury is such that it cannot be realised without misapprehension, limitation, and depreciation.

In fact, even in England, where the jury can of its own motion declare in the verdict its opinions, strictures, and suggestions of reform, as arising out of the trial, it is always subject to the guidance of the judge, and it is not employed in the less serious and most numerous cases, on which the whole decision is left to magistrates, who apparently are not to be trusted to decide upon crimes of a graver kind.

And as for the other political advantages of the jury, experience shows us that the jury is often more injurious than serviceable to liberty.

In the first place, in continental States the jury is but an institution artificially grafted, by a stroke of the pen, on the organism of the law, and has no vital connection or common roots with this and other social organisms, as it has in England. Also the example of classical antiquity is opposed to the institution of the jury, which has been imposed upon us by eager imitation and political symmetry; for if the jury had disappeared amongst continental nations, this simply means that it did not find in the ethnic types, the manners and customs, the physical and social environments of these nations, an adequate supply of vitality, such as it has retained, for instance through so many historical changes, amongst the Anglo-Saxons.

And if sometimes the jury can withstand the abuses of government, still too frequently it does not withstand its own passions, or the influence of the social class (the bourgeoisie in our own day), to which nearly all juries belong. It is notorious, in fact, that the jury is more rigorous in regard to prisoners accused of crimes against property than in regard to those accused of crimes against the person, especially crimes instigated by personal motives such as hate, vengeance, or the like; for every juryman thinks that he himself might be a victim of the exploits of a thief, or the attacks of a murderer for the sake of gain; whereas there is less reason to fear a murder provoked by vengeance, an outrage, an embezzlement of public money, or the like. And Machiavelli said that men would rather have blood drawn from their veins than money from their pockets.

Besides, the same jury which will resist pressure from the Government does not resist popular pressure, direct or indirect, especially in view of the secrecy of their individual votes. No doubt there are noble exceptions; but society is made up of average virtues, and only upon them can it count.[17]

[17] In Dublin, for the trial of the murderers of Burke and Lord Frederick Cavendish, in 1883, the empanelling of the jury was very difficult, for nobody was willing to expose himself to the vengeance of the fanatics.

And when it is continually asserted, in the words of Jouffroy, that the jury is an outpost of liberty, or in those of Carrara, that it is its necessary complement, we have to remark that this would be true if the jury were instituted by a despotic government; but when popular liberties have far more effectual guarantees in the political organisation of the State, then this quality of the jury is more apparent than real.

In fine, either the government is despotic, and then juries are not strong enough to preserve liberty, as in England from the time of Henry VIII. to that of James II.; or, as Mittermaier said, "when authority is corrupt, and the judge is cowardly or terrorised, a jury cannot assist in the defence of liberty." Or else the government is liberal, and then the judges also are independent, so that there is no need of juries, especially with the guarantees of their independence which I have already indicated.

Now history reminds us that the jury is never instituted by despotic governments. It was refused, for instance, in upper Italy by Napoleon in 1815, in Naples by the Bourbons in 1820, in Lombardy by Austria in 1849, and in our own day in Russia, for political crimes, though it is allowed for ordinary crimes.

Thus the jury, as a political and liberal institution, is oddly destined to be excluded when it would be serviceable, and to be useless when it is admitted. It reminds us of the destiny of the National Guard.

But, even in England, the jury is regarded as especially a legal institution; and the main qualities attributed to it in this connection are moral judgment and private conviction.

The law, we are told, has always a certain harshness and insufficiency, for it ought to provide for the future whilst grounding itself on the past, whereas it cannot foresee all possible cases. Progress is so rapid and manifold, in modern society, that penal laws cannot keep pace with it, even though they are frequently recast--as for instance in Bavaria, which in one century has had three penal codes, and in France, where an almost daily accumulation of special laws is piled upon the original text of the most ancient code in Europe.

The jury, by its moral judgment, corresponding in some degree to the equity of the ancients, is able to correct the summum jus with verdicts superior to the written law. And, in addition, the jury always follows its private conviction, the inspiration of sentiment, the voice of the conscience, pure instinct, in place of the stern and artificial maxims of the trained lawyer.

I do not deny these qualities of the jury; but I very much suspect that they are serious and dangerous vices rather than useful qualities in a legal institution.

In the first place, I believe that the distinction of powers or social functions, corresponding to the natural law of division of labour, ought not to be destroyed by the jury. The duty of the judicial power, before everything else, is to observe and apply the written law; for if we once admit the possibility that the judge (popular or trained) has to amend the law, all guarantee of liberty is lost, and the authority of the individual is unlimited. As I have said above, we allow the authority of the judge only when we have actual guarantees of his capacity and independence, and always within the limits of the general precepts of the law, and under the control of a superior disciplinary power.

But the omnipotence of the jury, liberated from all reasonable regulation, with no directing motives for its verdict, and no possibility of control, is a two-edged blade, which may sometimes improve upon the law, or at least usefully indicate to the legislator the tendencies of public opinion in regard to a particular crime. But it may also violate the law, and the liberty of the individual, and then we pay too dear for the slight advantage which the jury can confer, and which might be replaced by other manifestations of public opinion. In any case, as Bentham said, it is better to have our remedy in the law than in the subversion of the law.

As for private conviction, we willingly admit that no system of legal proof is acceptable. But it is one thing to substitute for the legal and artificial assurance of the law the assurance of the judge who tries the case, and quite another thing to substitute for conviction founded on argument, and for a critical examination of the evidence collected during the trial, the blind and simple promptings of instinct or sentiment.

Even apart from technical notions, which we consider necessary to the physio-psychological trial of any accused person, social justice certainly cannot be dispensed through the momentary and unconsidered impressions of a casual juryman. If a criminal trial consisted of the simple declaration that a particular action was good or bad, no doubt the moral consciousness of the individual would be sufficient; but since it is a question of the value of evidence and the examination of objective and subjective facts, moral consciousness does not suffice, and everything should be submitted to the critical exercise of the intellect.

To the instinctive blindness of the judgment of juries we must add their irresponsibility.

No doubt if the legislator required from all judges a simple Yes or No, then perhaps the jury would be as good as the magistrate. But instead of the unexplained verdict which Carmignani called ``the method of the cadi,'' we are of opinion that there should always be substituted a sentence based on reasons and capable of control, especially in the positive system of criminal procedure, which demands from the judge an acquaintance with anthropology and criminal sociology, and from his sentence the elements necessary to the subsequent treatment of the convict, in agreement with the characteristics of his individuality and of his crime.

But not only is the jury devoid of the qualities attributed to it; it has a fatal defect, which alone is sufficient to condemn this institution of the law.

In the first place, it is not easy to understand how a dozen jurymen, selected at hazard, can actually represent the popular conscience, which indeed frequently protests against their decisions. In any case, the fundamental conception of the jury is that the mere fact of its belonging to the people gives it the right to judge; and as the ancient assemblies are no longer possible, the essence of the jury is that chance alone must decide the practical exercise of this popular prerogative.

Now these two conceptions of the jury are in manifest contradiction with the universal rule of public end private life, that social functions should be exercised by persons selected as most capable.

Thus in everyday life we all require of every labourer the work of which he is more particularly capable. No one would dream, for instance, of having his watch mended by a cobbler. The administration of criminal justice, on the contrary, is demanded of any one we chance to come across, be he grocer or man of independent means, painter or pensioner, who may never in his life have witnessed a criminal trial!

The irregularity of our statutes corresponds to the incapacity of individual jurymen; for it is evident that we cannot impose the rigorous process of a special mode of procedure on the first- comer. And the law heightens the absurdity by plainly declaring that juries must give their decision without regard to the consequences of their verdict! ``Jurymen fail in their highest duty when they have regard to the penal law, and consider the consequences which their verdict may have upon the accused'' (Article 342 of the French code of criminal procedure).

That is to say, criminal justice should be based on the neglect of the elementary rule of justice, according to which every man ought always to consider the possible consequences of his actions. And the criminal law demands from juries this proof of their blindness (which is fortunately impossible) that they should judge blindfold, with no regard for the prisoner, or for the consequences which their verdict may have upon him.

It was impossible that the advocates of the jury should fail to see the absurdity of these principles; and they have been compelled to slur them over, at any rate in ordinary practice.

In respect of the composition of juries, restrictions have been introduced, by means of lists of eligible persons, selection by lot, the optional exclusion of a certain number of jurymen by the public prosecutor and the defence, &c. All these expedients, however, some of which are imposed by necessity, can only insure a general and presumptive capacity, for they have the merely negative effect of contributing to exclude the most manifest moral or intellectual incapacity. But the only capacity which is necessary in a judge, which is a special and positive capacity, is not guaranteed by these restrictions, which, after all, are a negation of the very principle of the jury.

And even if the jury were always composed of persons of adequate capacity, it would still be condemned by two inevitable arguments of human psychology.

First, the assembling of several individuals of typical capacity never affords a guarantee of collective capacity, for in psychology a meeting of individuals is far from being equivalent to the aggregate of their qualities. As in chemistry the combination of two gases may give us a liquid so in psychology the assembling of individuals of good sense may give us a body void of good sense. This is a phenomenon of psychological fermentation, by which individual dispositions, the least good and wise, that is the most numerous and effective, dominate the better ones, as the rule dominates the exceptions. This explains the ancient saying, ``The senators are good men, but the Senate is a mischievous animal."

And this fact of collective inferiority, not to say degeneracy, is observed in casual assemblies, such as juries, meetings, and the like, far more than in organised and permanent councils of judges, experts, &c.

Secondly, the jury, even when composed of persons of average capacity, will never be able in its judicial function to follow the best rules of intellectual evolution.

Human intelligence, in fact, both individual and collective, displays these three phases of progressive development: common sense, reason, and science, which are not essentially different, but which differ greatly in the degree of their complexity.

Now it is evident that a gathering of individuals of average capacity, but not technical capacity, will in its decisions only be able to follow the rules of common sense, or at most, by way of exception, the rules of reason--that is, of their common mental habits, more or less directed by a certain natural capacity. But the higher rules of science, which are still indispensable for a judgment so difficult as that which bears on crimes and criminals, will always be unknown to it.

As for the irregularity of the action of a jury, it has been deemed that this can be provided against by the formal distinction between a decision of fact and a decision of law, in obedience to the advice of Montesquieu, that ``to the popular judgment we should submit a single object, a fact, a single fact.''

But without dwelling on the remark of Hye-Glunek, that in this way the legal problem, which ought to be as indivisible as the syllogism which creates it, is cut into two parts, it is evident that Cambaceres was amply justified in saying, in the Council of State, that the separation of fact from law is a fallacy.

In fine, not only under the positive system of criminal procedure, which demands of the judge, in addition to legal conceptions of crime, some anthropological and sociological knowledge of criminals, but even at the present day it is more correct to say that the jury is concerned with the crime--that is, in the words of Binding, with a legal fact, and not merely a material fact; whilst the judge is concerned with the punishment. Thus, in the Assize Court, the separation of the judgments is not between fact and law, but only between the crime and the punishment

Even admitting the possibility of this separation of fact and law, logic and experience have already belied the assertion of those who say with Beccaria that, ``for the appreciation of facts, ordinary intelligence is better than science, common sense better than the highest mental faculties, and ordinary training better than scientific.''

On the contrary, a criminal trial is not only concerned with the direct perception of facts, but also and especially with their critical reconstruction and psychological appreciation. In civil law the fact is really accessory, and both sides may be agreed in its exposition, whilst disputing about the application of the law to this fact. But in criminal justice the fact is the principal element, and it is not merely necessary to admit or to decide upon this or that detail, but we have also to regard its causes and effects, from the individual and the social point of view, without speaking of the common difficulty of a critical and evidential appreciation of a mass of significant circumstances. So that, as Ellero said, in a criminal trial the decision as to fact is far more difficult than that as to law. And by this time daily practice has accumulated so many proofs, more or less scandalous, of the incapacity of the jury even to appreciate facts, that it is useless to dwell upon them.

To conclude this question of the jury, it remains to speak of its defects, which are not the more or less avoidable consequences of a more or less fortunate application of the principle, which might be the case with any social institution, but, on the contrary, are an inevitable consequence of the laws of psychology and sociology.

So far as science is concerned, a fact exists in connection with a general law. For common sense, on the other hand, the actuality of the particular fact is the only matter of concern. Hence the inevitable tendency of the jury to be dominated by isolated facts, with no other guide than sentiment, which, especially in southern races, confines all pity to the criminals, whilst the crime and its victims are all but forgotten. The very keenness of sentiment which would urge the people to administer ``summary justice'' on the criminal, when surprised in the fact, turns entirely in his favour when he is brought up at the assizes, with downcast mien, several months after the crime. Hence we obtain an impassioned and purblind justice.

And the predominance of sentiment over the intelligence of the jury is revealed in the now incurable aspect of judicial discussions. There is no need and no use for legal and sociological studies and for technical knowledge; the only need is for oratorical persuasiveness and sentimental declamations. Thus we have heard an advocate telling a jury that, ``in trials into which passion enters, we must decide with passion.'' Hence, also, the deterioration of science in the Assize Courts, and its faulty application, and its completely erroneous consequences.

Moreover, the verdict of the jury cannot represent the sum of spontaneous and individual convictions--not only in countries where juries are exposed to all kinds of influences during the adjournments of the discussion, but even in England, where unanimity is required, and where all communication of the jury with the outer world is forbidden until the end of the trial. For in every case the influence of the most intriguing or most respected jurymen in the jury's room is always inevitable. So that we have even had irresponsible suggestions of public deliberation on the part of the jury.

Against these defects of the jury its advocates have set an objection in regard to the trained judge, namely that the habit of judging crimes and offences irresistibly inclines the judge to look upon every prisoner as guilty, and to extinguish the presumption of innocence even in cases where it would be most justified.

This objection has really a psychological basis; for the conversion of the conscious into the unconscious, and the polarisation of the intellectual faculties and dispositions, are facts of daily observation, determined by the biological law of the economy of force. But it is not sufficient to make us prefer juries to judges.

In addition to the fact that this mental habit of judges may be counteracted by a better selection of magistrates under the reforms which I have indicated, it is to be observed that this presumption of innocence, as we have seen, is not so absolute as some would have us believe, especially in case of a trial which follows upon a series of inquiries and proofs in; the preliminary hearing.

Again, this tendency of judges is restrained and corrected by the publicity of the discussions. And all, or nearly all, the famous and oft-repeated instances of judicial errors go back to the time of the inquisitorial and secret trial--in regard to which an interesting historical problem presents itself; that is to say the co-existence of the inquisitorial trial, which impairs every individual guarantee, with the political liberties of the mediaeval Italian republics.

This is why the number of acquittals, and of the admission of extenuating circumstances, is always very remarkable, even in the Correctional Tribunals, which in Italy show proportions not greatly differing from those of the Assize Courts.

We must remember that, under our modern penal procedure, it is not the individual guarantees that are lacking, such as the assigning of reasons for the sentence, the almost total abolition of punishments which cannot be reconsidered, appeals, reversals, revision, which would be still more efficacious under the positive system which we propose.

One logical consequence of the psychological objection raised against judges would be the granting of a jury even in the Correctional Tribunals, though the experience which we have of it in the Assize Courts is not so encouraging as to leave many advocates of a jury in the minor courts.

But a decisive objection, founded on the most positive data of sociology, can be raised against the jury.

The law of natural evolution proves that no variation in the vegetable or animal organism is useful or durable which is not the outcome of a slow and gradual preparation by organic forces and external conditions. Thus an organ which ceases to have a function to discharge is subject to atrophy, and no new organ is possible or capable of development if it is not required by a new function to which it corresponds.

What has been said of organic variations is also true of social institutions. And when the jury is contemplated from this point of view, we see that it has been artificially grafted by a stroke of the legislator's pen on the judicial institutions of the continent, without the long-continued, spontaneous and organic connections which it had, for instance, with the English people. The jury had even disappeared from the continental countries in which it had left traces of former existence; for it had not found in the race-characteristics or the social organism that favourable environment which is supplied in England by the natural groundwork of institutions and principles which, as Mittermaier says, are its necessary correlative.

The jury, as it has been politically established on the continent of Europe, is what Spencer calls a false membrane in the social organism, having no physiological connection with the rest of the body politic. So that it is not yet acclimatised, even in France, after a century of uninterrupted trial.[18]

[18] The actual state of the law in Europe, so far as regards the jury for common crimes and offences, is as follows:--England, Scotland, Ireland, and Switzerland have the jury for assizes and courts of first instance. France, Italy, Cisleithan Austria, Istria, Dalmatia, Rhenish Prussia, Alsace-Lorraine, Bavaria, Bohemia, Gallicia, Belgium, Roumania, Greece, Portugal, Russia, and Malta, have the criminal jury only. Spain had suspended it, but restored it in 1888. Prussia, Saxony, Baden, Wurtemberg, have the criminal jury and echevins (bodies of citizens sitting with the judges) for correctional and police cases. Denmark, Sweden, and Finland, have the echevins. Holland, Norway, Hungary, Slavonia, Poland, Servia, and Turkey, have neither juries nor echevins.

As for the other bio-sociological law, of single organs for single functions, it seems to me that if in England the jury and the magistracy have been developed side by side and interwoven, this is only a case of organic integration. But on the continent, as the jury has been added artificially to the magistracy, this is on the other hand a genuine example of non-natural growth.

And if it be said that the jury, as an advance from the homogeneous to the heterogeneous, indicates a higher degree of social evolution, we must draw a distinction between differentiations which amount to evolution and those which, on the contrary, are symptoms of dissolution. Division of labour, physiological or social, is a true evolutionary differentiation; whilst modifications introduced by a disease in the animal organism, or by a revolt in the social organism, are but the beginning of a more or less extended dissolution.

Now the jury belongs to the domain of social pathology, for it is essentially contrary to the law of the specialisation of functions, according to which every organ which becomes more adapted to a given task is no longer adapted to any other. It is only in the lower organisms that the same tissue or organ can perform different functions, whilst in the vertebrates the stomach can only serve for digestion, the lungs for oxygenation, and so on. Similarly in primitive societies, each individual is soldier, hunter, tiller of the soil, &c., whilst with the progress of social evolution every man performs his special function, and becomes unfitted for other labours. In the jury we have a return to the primitive confusion of social functions, by giving to any chance comer, who may be an excellent labourer, or artist, a very delicate judicial function, for which he has no capacity to-day, and will have no available experience to-morrow.

In modern societies, to tell the truth, there is another function assigned to all citizens, outside of their special capacity, and that is the electoral duty. But the cases are very different. The franchise does not demand a labour so difficult and delicate as critical judgment, and the reconstruction of the conditions of an act and of its author. It has no direct influence on the positive function of the person elected, but on the contrary it is a confession of the special incapacity of the elector to do what he intrusts to the capacity of the person elected. The franchise is but an elementary function of the assimilation of physiological elements in the social organism, which in the animal organism is performed by the aggregate of living cells, and in society by the aggregate of individuals, not being idiots or criminals, who possess the minimum of social energy.

Far different is the administration of criminal justice, a technical and very noble function, which has nothing in common with the elementary function of the franchise. I could not indeed agree with the assertion of Carrara, who thought it a contradiction to deny to the people any participation in the exercise of the judicial authority when they are allowed to participate in the exercise of legislative authority. In the first place, the people have but a very indirect share in the legislative function, and, even where the referendum exists, very useful as I believe it to be, the people have only a simple, almost negative function, to say Yes or No to a law which they have not made, and would have had no technical ability to make. Thus the argument of Carrara could only lead to the popular election of judges, as of legislators, and to a control by the people of the administrative action of the judges when elected No doubt this would have theoretical advantages, though in my opinion it would raise practical difficulties, especially in nations which do not possess a very keen conscience and political activity, after enfeeblement by centuries of despotism, or of political and administrative tutelage and centralisation.

The jury, then, is a retrogressive institution, as shown by history and sociology, for it represents the mediaeval and instinctive phase of criminal justice. It has, indeed, a few advantages (there is always a certain profit in misfortune), especially when it operates on the final outcome of the classical theories--bringing to bear, for instance, an irresistible force against repeated theft, or murders committed at the instigation of others. And it has sometimes drawn attention to necessary penal reforms, after accepting certain conclusions of the positive school, such as the acquittal of criminals of passion, and political prisoners, or a greater severity towards habitual criminals.

But the only possible conclusion from the foregoing criticisms is that the jury should be abolished for the trial of common crimes, AFTER the introduction of reforms which would ensure the capacity and independence of the judges.

Meanwhile, since it is much easier to establish a new social institution than to abolish one, it is worth while to indicate the principal and most urgent reforms which should be made in the jury system, so as to eliminate its more serious and frequent disadvantages.

The theoretical distinction of the classical school between ordinary and political crimes is not very precise, for the so- called political crimes are either not crimes (as when they are confined to the manifestation of an idea), or they are common crimes which spring from a lofty and social passion in individuals, who have the characteristics of the criminal by passion, or, in other words,--are but quasi-criminals; or else they are common crimes committed by ordinary malefactors, under the pretext of a popular idea. Instead of distinguishing crimes, I think we ought to distinguish between ordinary and political criminals, according to their determining motives, and the social bearings and historical moment of their acts. At the same time, whilst our criminal laws retain this distinction, I think it is useful to keep the jury for the trial of political crimes and offences, and for those connected with the press and with society as a whole; for if in these cases the jury might yield to the influence of class interests and prejudices (as for instance in the trial of actions arising out of the conflict of capital and labour), the danger will still be less than it would be with judges alone, who are not sufficiently independent of the executive, which in its turn is but the secular arm of the dominant class, and which therefore combines the interests and prejudices of the political order with those of the economic and moral order which dominate the jury.

For common crimes it would be necessary to withhold from a jury the trial of prisoners who avow their crime. The essence of a trial by indictment is the principle that the discussion as to punishment is a private affair, and it has no further ground for existence when one of the parties withdraws from the duel. Hence the English mistrust of a prisoner's confession of guilt, which in the inquisitorial trial, on the other hand, is a mainstay of the evidence. Yet I believe that in these cases the Scottish system is preferable to the English. In England the judge begins by asking the prisoner if he is Guilty or Not Guilty, and in case of a confession he passes sentence without a verdict from the jury. In Scotland, on the contrary, the prosecutor can furnish his proof, in spite of the confession of the prisoner, and demand a verdict from the jury. In this way it is possible to avoid not only a scandalous acquittal of prisoners who have confessed their guilt (as happens in Italy, France, and elsewhere), but also the danger that the confession may not be true, and that an innocent man may be condemned.

Juries ought, moreover, as proposed by M. Ellero, to specify attenuating circumstances, on each of which a special question ought to be put to them.

The jury ought also to have the right of spontaneously finding in a sense less serious than that of the charge, even when no corresponding question has been put to them.

But at the same time it cannot be denied that these would only be palliatives, more or less efficacious.

The only positive conclusion is that, whilst retaining the jury for crimes of the political and social order, we should aim at its abolition for common crimes, immediately after securing stringent reforms as to the independence and capacity of the judges.

IV.

It needs no further demonstration that the modern organisation of punishment, based partly on the assumption that we can measure the moral culpability of criminals, and partly on an illusion as to their general amendment, and almost entirely reduced, in consequence, to imprisonment and the cell system, has absolutely failed to protect society against crime.

Holtzendorff, one of the best known of the classical school, frankly confessed that "the prison systems have made shipwreck." So also in Italy we have had disquisitions "on the futility of repression," and in Germany it has been held that "existing criminal law is powerless against crime." Thus the necessity of taking steps to counteract this failure is forced upon us more and more every day. We must proceed either by way of legislative reforms, as effectual as we can make them, but always inspired by reaction against the established prison system, or by a propaganda on scientific lines. The most striking form which has been taken by the latter process is the International Union of Penal Law, which in 1891, two years after its foundation, numbered nearly six hundred members of various nationalities, and which in the second clause of its charter, in spite of the varied reservations of a few members, notably supported the positive theories.

The defects of the penal system inspired by the theories of the classical school of criminal law, and by the actual regulations of the classical prison school, may be briefly summed up. They are, a fallacious scale of moral responsibility; absolute ignorance and neglect of the physio-psychological types of criminals; intervals between verdict and sentence on the one hand, and between the sentence and its execution on the other, with a consequent abuse of pardons; disastrous practical effects of corruption and of criminal association in prisons; millions of persons condemned to short terms of imprisonment, which are foolish and absurd; and a continuous, inexorable increase of recidivism.

113

So that the tribunals of Europe, as M. Prins observed, with the absolute impersonality of modern justice, allow their sentences to fall upon unhappy wretches as a tap allows water to fall drop by drop upon the ground.

Without counting fines or police detention, there were sentenced in Italy, in the ten years 1880-89, to various terms of imprisonment, 587,938 persons by the Pretors, and 465,130 by the Correctional Tribunals. That is, more than a million terms in the minor courts within ten years!

And the total number sentenced in Italy to various punishments, by Pretors, Tribunals, and Assize Courts, in the same ten years, was not less than 3,230,000.

As for recidivism, without repeating the familiar figures of its annual increase, it will suffice to recall the astounding fact to which I drew attention before the central Commission of Legal Judicial Statistics. That is to say, amongst the prisoners condemned in 1887 for simple homicide, there were 224 who had been already condemned, either FOR THE SAME CRIME (63), or for a crime mentioned in the same section of the penal code (181); and even of those condemned for qualified manslaughter, 78 had already been condemned, either FOR THE SAME CRIME (8), or for one of like character.

In France we have figures equally striking, for they relate not to the effect of exceptional conditions, or conditions peculiar to this or that country, but to the uniform consequence of the classical theories of criminal law and prison organisation.

The total number condemned to imprisonment by the French tribunals, and detained by the police, in the ten years 1879-88, was 1,675,000; the Tribunal sentences under six days being 113,000.

And the total condemned to punishments of various kinds, by Assize Courts, Tribunals, and police courts, reached in the same ten years the enormous number of 6,440,000 individuals!

The meaning of this is that penal justice at the present moment is a vast machine, devouring and casting up again an enormous number of individuals, who lose amongst its wheels their life, their honour, their moral sense, and their health, bearing thenceforth the ineffaceable scars, and falling into the ever-growing ranks of professional crime and recidivism, too often without a hope of recovery.[19]

[19] As regards recidivism and the enormous numbers tried, England is in as bad a position as Italy and France. See my articles in Nineteenth Century, 1892, and Fortnightly Review, 1894.--ED.

It is impossible, then, to deny the urgent necessity of substituting for our present penal organisation a better system corresponding to the governing conditions of crime, more effectual for social defence, and at the same time less gratuitously disastrous for the individuals with whom it deals.

The positive school, in addition to the partial reforms proposed by Lombroso, and by myself in the second edition of this work, has put forward in the Criminology of Garofalo a ``rational system of punishment," whereof it is desirable to give a summary.

I. MURDERERS (moral insensibility and instinctive cruelty) who commit--

Murder for greed, or other selfish

gratification Criminal Lunatic Asylums: or

Murder unprovoked by the victim the death penalty. Murder with attendant cruelty

II. VIOLENT OR IMPULSIVE CHARACTERS (deficiency of the sense of pity, with prejudices on the subject of honour, on the duty of revenge, &c.). Adults who commit--

Violent assault suddenly provoked Removal of the offender from the

by a cruel injury neighbourhood of the victim or

Justifiable homicide in self-defence his family.

Transportation to an island, colony

Homicide to avenge honour or village--at liberty, under (isolated or endemic) supervision (for an indefinite

period, with from 5 to 10 years supervision).

Bodily injury during a quarrel; Damages and fine: heavy for such

slight and transitory malice; as can pay. Alternative
blows; threats; slander; verbal penalty:--deduction from wages,
insults or forced labour. Imprisonment

in case of refusal.

Malicious injury or disfigurement; Criminal lunatic asylum (for

mutilation; rape or outrage with hysterical or epileptic), or
violence; restraint on personal Transportation for an indefinite
liberty period, with supervision from 5
to 10 years.

Young persons who commit-- Criminal lunatic asylums (for

those with congenital

Crimes of violence without excuse, tendencies).

or rape Penal colony in case of relapse.
Transportation without constraint.

III. DISHONEST CRIMINALS. Adults who commit-- Habitual theft, swindling,
incendiarism, Lunatic asylums (if insane or

forgery, extortion epileptic). Transportation.
Labour-gangs (unfixed periods);

Occasional theft; swindling; or suspension of right to exercise forgery; extortion;
incendiarism a profession, until complete

reparation of damage.

Peculation; embezzlement; sale of Loss of office. Suspension of

offices; abuse of authority civil rights. Fine. Restitution.

Incendiarism; vindictive destruction Reparation of damage (with optional of
property (without personal imprisonment). Criminal injury) lunatic asylums (for the
insane).

Transportation (for recidivists).

Bankruptcy, when due to malpractice Restitution. Prohibition to trade

116

or to discharge public functions.

Uttering false coin; forgery of stock Imprisonment (unfixed periods) and certificates; personation, and fine, in addition to loss of false witness, &c. office, and restitution.

Bigamy, palming or concealment of Banishment for unfixed periods.

birth

Young persons who commit-- Theft, swindling, &c. An agricultural colony (for unfixed

periods).

IV. Persons guilty of--

Outbreaks, resistance or disobedience Imprisonment(for unfixed periods)

to authority

In other words, the system of repression proposed by M. Garofalo amounts to this:--

Absolute elimination of the criminal

Penalty of death
Criminal lunatic asylum.
Transportation with liberty.
Perpetual banishment.

Relative elimination Banishment for various periods.

Agricultural colonies.
Interdiction from a particular
neighbourhood.

By payment of money.

Reparation of damages Deduction from wages. Fine (going to the State) Forced labour, without Indemnification of the victims imprisonment.

Imprisonment for fixed periods for special offences (forgery and outbreaks);

or as alternative to indemnification or forced labour.

Interdiction of certain professions and public functions.

M. Liszt also, agreeing with the positive school in regard to the necessity of a radical reform in the penal system, yet with certain reservations, has propounded a scheme, which, however, as it does not sufficiently consider various classes of criminals, whom he divides merely into the habitual and the occasional, would need completion, especially in comparison with the well-reasoned scheme of Garofalo. M. Liszt's system is as follows:--

Punishment by fines.

In proportion to the property of the

offender--not alternative with For offences (with alternative imprisonment imprisonment).

Capable of being worked out by For contraventions of the law

forced labour without imprisonment (without imprisonment).

Conditional sentences.

For first offenders condemned to

imprisonment, with or without For offences punishable by sureties for three years imprisonment.

Imprisonment (for an indeterminate period, a maximum and minimum being enacted). Separate confinement--six weeks to two years.

House of detention (separate for 2 to 15 years (with police

one year, then gradual relaxation supervision and assistance of discharged prisoners)--or for life.

Indemnifications (always as a civil liability) added to other penalties.

I believe, however, that it is necessary, before laying down practical and detailed schemes, more or less complete, to establish certain general criteria, based upon the anthropological, physical, and social data of crime, such as may lead up to a positive system of social defence.

These fundamental criteria, it seems to me, can be reduced to the three following:--(1) No fixity in the periods of segregation of criminals; (2) the social and public character of the exaction of damages; (3) the adaptation of defensive measures to the various types of criminals.

1. For every crime which is committed, the problem of punishment ought no longer to consist in administering a particular dose, as being proportionate to the moral culpability of the criminal; but it should be limited to the question whether by the actual conditions (breach of law or infliction of injury) and by the personal conditions (the anthropological type of the criminal) it is necessary to separate the offender from his social environment for ever, or for a longer or shorter period, according as he is or is not regarded as capable of being restored to society, or whether it is sufficient to exact from him a strict reparation of the injury which he has inflicted.

Under this head there is a radical contradiction. The existing schemes of punishment, differing in their machinery (and out of harmony with the sentence of the judge, often even with the terms of the law), are all based on the principle of fixed periods of punishment, graduated into hundreds and thousands of possible doses, and have regard far more to the crime than to the criminal. On the other hand we have the positive system of punishment, based on the principle of an unfixed segregation of the criminal, which is a logical consequence of the theory that punishment ought not to be the visitation of a crime by a retribution, but rather a defence of society adapted to the danger personified by the criminal.

This principle of unfixed punishment is not new, but it is only the positive theory which has given it system and life. The idea of justice as assigning punishment to a crime, measured out by days and weeks, is too much opposed to the principle of the indeterminate sentence to allow it to receive any systematic trial under the sway of the classical theories. There has been only an isolated and exceptional use of it here and there, such as the seclusion of mad criminals in special asylums, ``during her Majesty's pleasure," in England. Nevertheless, personal freedom (which is held to be violated by seclusion for unfixed periods) is greatly respected by the English people.

The fundamental principle of law is that of a restriction imposed by the necessity of social existence. It is evident, therefore, to begin with, that seclusion for an unfixed period, as for life, is in no way irreconcilable with this principle of law, when imposed by necessity. Thus it has been proposed, even by the classical school, as a mode of compensation or adjustment.

119

If, indeed, we admit an increase of punishment for a first relapse, it is logical that this increase should be proportional to the number of relapses, until we come to perpetual seclusion or transportation, and even to death, as under the mediaeval laws. So that there are some of the classical school who, by way of being logical if not practical, and refusing to admit progressive increase, begin by refusing increase in any degree, even for a first relapse.

Moreover, if the jurists agree in allowing conditional liberation, before the term assigned in the sentence, when the prisoner seems to have given proof of amendment, the natural consequence, by mere abstract logic, ought to be a prolongation of punishment for the prisoner who is not amended, but continues to be dangerous.

This is admitted, amongst others, by Ortolan, Davesies de Pontes, and Roeder, who quote as favourable, though only for recidivists, Henke Stelzer, Reichmann, Mohl, Groos, von Struve, von Lichtenberg, Gotting, Krause, Ahrens, Lucas Bonneville, Conforti, and others, amongst students of criminality; and Ducpetiaux, Ferrus, Thomson, Mooser, Diez, Valentini, and D'Alinge amongst prison experts.

After this first period, the principle of segregation for an unfixed term, as a basis for the penal system, has been supported by Despine, and developed by a few German writers. These latter have insisted especially on the disadvantages of the penal systems inspired by the classical theories, though they run somewhat to excess, like Mittelstadt, who proposed the re- establishment of the brutal punishment of flogging.

In corporal punishments, it is true, there would be a certain gain of efficaciousness, particularly against such hardened offenders as the born criminals, so that there is a reaction in favour of these punishments. M. Roncati, for instance, writing of prison hygiene, says that he would be glad to see ``the maternal regime,'' with its salutary use of physical pain before the child has developed a moral sense; and if flogging is objectionable, resort might be had to electricity, which is capable of giving pain without being dangerous to health or revolting. Similarly Bain says that the physiological theory of pleasure and pain has a close relation to that of rewards and punishments, and that, as punishment ought to be painful, so long as it does not injure the convict's health (which imprisonment is just as likely to do), we might have recourse to electric shocks, which frighten the subject by their mysterious power, without being repugnant. Again, the English Commission of Inquiry into the results of the law of penal servitude declared in its report that, ``In English prisons, disciplinary corporal punishments (formerly the lash, then the birch) are inflicted only for the most serious offences. The evidence has shown that in many cases they produce good results.''

Nevertheless corporal punishments, as the main form of repression, even when carried out with less barbarous instruments, are too deeply opposed to the sentiment of humanity to be any longer possible in a penal code. At the same time they are admissible as disciplinary punishments, under the form of cold baths, electric shocks, &c., all the more because, whether prescribed by law or not, they are inevitable in prisons, and, when not regulated by law, give rise to many abuses, as was shown at the Stockholm Prison Conference in 1878.

I agree with Kirchenheim that Dr. Kraepelin's scheme of seclusion for unfixed periods is more practical and hopeful. When the measure of punishment is fixed beforehand, the judge, as Villert says, ``is like a doctor who, after a superficial diagnosis, orders a draft for the patient, and names the day when he shall be sent out of hospital, without regard to the state of his health at the time.'' If he is cured before the date fixed, he must still remain in the hospital; and he must go when the time is up, cured or not.

Semal reached the same conclusion in his paper on ``conditional liberation,'' at the second Congress of Criminal Anthropology.

And this notion of segregation for unfixed periods, put forward in 1867 for incorrigible criminals by the Swiss Prison Reform Association, has already made great progress, especially in England and America, since the Prison Congress of London (1872) discussed this very question of indefinite sentences, which the National Prison Congress at Cincinnati had approved in the preceding year.

In 1880 M. Garofalo and I both spoke in favour of indefinite segregation, though only for incorrigible recidivists; and the same idea was strikingly supported in M. Van Hamel's speech at the Prison Congress at Rome (1885). The eloquent criminal expert of Amsterdam, speaking ``on the discretion which should be left to the judge in awarding punishment,'' made a primary distinction between habitual criminals, incorrigible and corrigible, and occasional criminals. ``For the first group, perpetual imprisonment should depend on certain conditions fixed by law, and on the decision of the judge after a further inquiry. For the second group, the application of an undefined punishment after the completion of the first sentence will have to depend in the graver cases on the conditions laid down by law, and in less serious cases upon the same conditions together with the decision of the judge, who will always decide from time to time, after further inquiry, as to the necessity for prolonging the imprisonment. For the third group, the judge will have to be limited by law, in deciding the punishment, by special maximums, and with a general minimum.''

The Prison Congress of Rome naturally did not accept the principle of punishment for unfixed periods. More than that, advancing on the classical tendency, it decided that ``the law should fix the maximum of punishment beyond which the judge may not in any case go; and also the minimum, which however may be diminished when the judge considers that the crime was accompanied by extenuating circumstances not foreseen by the law."

It is only of late years, in consequence of the reaction against short terms of imprisonment, that the principle of segregation for unfixed periods has been developed and accepted by various writers, in spite of the feeble objections of Tallack, Wahlberg, Lamezan, von Jagemann, &c.

Apart, also, from theoretical discussion, this principle has been applied in a significant manner in the United States, by means of the ``indeterminate sentence." The House of Correction at Elmira (New York) for young criminals carries into effect, with special regulations of physical and moral hygiene, the indeterminate imprisonment of young prisoners; and this principle, approved by the Prison Congresses at Atlanta (1887), Buffalo (1888), and Nashville (1889), has been applied also in the New York prisons, and in the States of Massachusetts, Pennsylvania, Minnesota, and Ohio.

M. Liszt proposes that the indeterminate character of punishment should be only relative, that is to say, limited between a minimum and a maximum, these being laid down in the sentence of the judge. Special commissions for supervising the administration of punishment, consisting of the Governor of the prison, the Public Prosecutor, the judge who heard the case, and two members nominated by Government (instead of the court which passed sentence, as proposed by Villert and Van Hamel), should decide on the actual duration of the punishment, after having examined the convict and his record. Thus these commissions would be able to liberate at once (with or without conditions) or to order a prolongation of punishment, especially for habitual criminals.

With the formation of these commissions there might be associated the prison studies and aid of discharged prisoners referred to on a former page.

But I think that this proposal of M. Liszt is acceptable only for commissions of supervision, or of the execution of punishment, such as already exist in several countries, with a view solely to prison administration and benevolence, and in which of course the experts of criminal anthropology ought to take part, who, as I have suggested, should be included in every preliminary criminal inquiry. As for the determination of the maximum and minimum in such a sentence, I believe it would not be practicable; the acting commissions might find it necessary to go beyond them, and it would be opposed to the very principle of indeterminate segregation. The reason given by M. Liszt, that with this provision the contrast with actual systems of punishment would be less marked, does not seem to me decisive; for the principle we maintain is so radically opposed to traditional theories and to legislative and judicial custom that this optional passing of the limits would avoid no difficulty, whilst it would destroy the advantages of the new system.

In other words, when the conditions of the act committed and the criminal who has committed it show that the reparation of the damage inflicted is not sufficient by way of a defensive measure, the judge will only have to pronounce in his sentence an indefinite detention in the lunatic asylum, the prison for incorrigibles, or the establishments for occasional criminals (penal colonies, &c.).

The execution of this sentence will be rendered definite by successive steps, which will no longer be detached, as they now are, from the action of the magistrate, and taken without his knowledge, but will be a systematic continuation of his work. Permanent commissions for the supervision of punishment, composed of administrative functionaries, experts in criminal anthropology, magistrates, and representatives of the Public Prosecutor and the defence, would render impossible that desertion and oblivion of the convict which now follow almost immediately on the delivery of the sentence, with the execution of which the judge has nothing to do, except to see that he is represented. Pardon, or conditional liberation, or the serving of the full punishment, are all left at present to the chance of a blind official routine. These commissions would have great social importance, for they would mean on one hand the protection of society against imprudent liberation of the most dangerous criminals, and on the other hand the protection of the less dangerous against the danger of an imprisonment recognised as excessive and unnecessary.

Allied to the principle of indeterminate segregation is that of conditional release, which with the progressive prison system, known as the Irish, is now accepted in nearly all European countries. But conditional liberation in the system of definite punishments, without distinction amongst the types of criminals, is both contradictory in theory and ineffectual in practice. At present, indeed, it has only a mechanical and almost impersonal application, with one fallacious test, that of the alleged ``good conduct" of the prisoner, which, according to the English Inquiry Commission in 1863, ``can only have the negative value of the absence of grave breaches of discipline."

It will be understood that conditional release, as it would be organised in the positive system of indeterminate segregation, ought only to be granted after a physio-psychological examination of the prisoner, and not after an official inspection of documents, as at present. So that it will be refused, no longer, as now, almost exclusively in regard to the gravity of the crime, but in regard to the greater or less re-adaptability of the criminal to social conditions. It will therefore be necessary to deny it to mad and born criminals who are guilty of great crimes.

Conditional liberation is now carried out under the special supervision of the police; but this is an ineffectual measure for crafty criminals, and disastrous for occasional criminals, who are shut out by the supervision from re-adaptation to normal existence. The system of indeterminate segregation renders all special supervision useless. Moreover, this duty only distracts policemen by compelling them to keep an eye on a few hundred liberated convicts, and to neglect thousands of other criminals, who increase the number of unknown perpetrators of crime.

Similarly as to the discharged prisoners' aid societies, which, notwithstanding their many sentimental declamations, and the excellence of their intentions, continue to be as sterile as they are benevolent. The reason here also is that they forget to take into account the different types of criminals, and that they are accustomed to give their patronage impartially to all discharged prisoners, whether they are reclaimable or not. It must not be forgotten, moreover, that this aiding of malefactors ought not to be exaggerated when there are millions of honest workmen more unfortunate than these liberated prisoners. In spite of all the sentimentalism of the prisoners' aid societies, I believe that a foreman will always be in the right if he chooses an honest workman for a vacancy in his workshops in preference to a discharged prisoner.

At the same time these societies may produce good results if they concern themselves solely with occasional criminals, and especially with the young, and make their study of crime contribute to the training of future magistrates and pleaders.

2. The second fundamental principle of the positive system of social defence against crime is that of indemnification for damage, on which the positive school has always dwelt, in combination with radical, theoretical, and practical reforms.

Reparation of damage suffered by the victims of crime may be regarded from three different points of view:--(1) As an obligation of the criminal to the injured party; (2) as an alternative for imprisonment for slight offences committed by occasional criminals; and (3) as a social function of the State on behalf of the injured person, but also in the indirect and not less important interest of social defence.

The positive school has affirmed the last two reforms--the second on the initiative of Garofalo and Puglia, and the third on my own proposal, which, as being more radical, has been more sharply contested by the classical and eclectic schools.

In my treatise on ``The Right of Punishment as a Social Function,'' I said: ``Let us not be told that civil reparation is no part of penal responsibility. I can see no real difference between the payment of a sum of money as a fine and its payment as damages; but more than that, I think a mistake has been made in separating civil and penal measures too absolutely, whereas they ought to be conjoined for defensive purposes, in preventing certain particular anti-social acts." And again, classifying the measures of social defence (``measures of prevention, reparation, repression, and elimination"), I said in regard to measures of reparation: ``Our proposed reform is not intended to be theoretical merely, for indeed it may be said already that this liability to indemnify is established in the majority of cases; but it should be above all a practical reform, in the sense that, instead of separating civil and penal measures, we shall make their joint application more certain, and even require special regulations to compel the criminal judges, for instance, to assess the damages, and so avoid the delays and mischances of a new trial before the civil judges, and to compel the Public Prosecutor to make an official demand, even when through ignorance or fear there is no action on the part of the injured person, that the criminal should be condemned to make good the loss which he has inflicted. It will then be seen that the fear of having to make strict restitution will be a spur to the diligence of the well-to-do, in regard to involuntary offences, whilst for the poor we shall be able to impose work on behalf of the injured person in place of pecuniary damages."

Shortly afterwards Garofalo wrote: ``In the opinion of our school, for many offences, especially slighter offences against the person, it would be serviceable to substitute for a few days' imprisonment an effectual indemnification of the injured party. Reparation of damage might become a genuine penal substitute, when instead of being, as now, a legal consequence, a right which can be enforced by the rules of civil procedure, it would become an obligation from which the accused could in no way extract himself."

Of all the positive school, Garofalo has insisted most strongly on these ideas, enlarging upon them in various proposals for the practical reform of procedure.

The principle has made further progress since the speech of M. Fioretti at the first Congress of Criminal Anthropology (Rome, 1885), which adopted the resolution brought forward by MM. Ferri, Fioretti, and Venezian: ``The Congress, being convinced of the importance of providing for civil indemnification, in the immediate interest, not only of the injured party, but also of preventive and repressive social defence, is of opinion that legislation could most expeditiously enact the most suitable measures against such as cause loss to other persons, and against their accomplices and abettors, by treating the recovery of damages as a social function assigned to its officials, that is to say, to the Public Prosecutor at the bar, to the judges in their sentences, to the prison officials in the ultimate payment for prison labour, and in the stipulation for conditional release."

The classical principle that indemnification for loss caused by an unlawful act is a purely civil and private obligation of the offender (like that created by any breach of contract!), and that in consequence it ought to be essentially distinct from the penal sentence which is a public reparation, has inevitably caused the complete oblivion of indemnification in every-day judicial practice. For the victims of crime, finding themselves compelled to resort to the courts, and fearing the expense of a civil trial to give effect to the sentence of damages and interest thereon, have been driven to abandon the hope of seeing their loss actually and promptly compensated. Hence the necessity for some paltry compromise, which has to be accepted almost as a generous concession from the offender, together with the revival of private vengeance, and a loss of confidence in the reparatory action of social justice.

Even in the scientific domain it has come about that criminal experts have abandoned the question of indemnification to the civil experts, and these in their turn have almost suffered it to pass into oblivion, inasmuch as they always regarded it as belonging to matters of penal law and procedure.

It is only by the radical innovation of the positive school that this legal custom has received new energy and vitality.

I do not, however, intend in this place to concern myself with indemnification from the first point of view, namely, the forms of procedure necessary to render it more strict and effectual, such as the official demand and execution by the Public Prosecutor, even when no action is brought by the injured party; the fixing of the damages in every penal sentence; the immediate lien and claim upon the goods of the condemned person, so as to avoid the pretence of inability to pay; the paying down of the sum, or a part of the salary or wages of solvent defendants; compulsory labour by those unable to pay; the assignment of part of the prison wages for the benefit of the victims; the payment of all or most of the damages as a necessary condition of pardon or conditional release; the establishment of a treasury of fines for prepayment to the family of the victims; the liability of the heirs of the condemned persons for indemnifications, and so forth.

All these propositions are in sharp contrast with Art. 37 of the new Italian penal code, which has given no other guarantee to the victims of offences than the superfluous, or ironical, or immoral declaration that ``penal condemnation does not prejudice the right of the injured person to restitution and indemnification"--as though there were any doubt of the fact.

I only wish to insist on the question of principle, that is, on the essentially public character which we assign to indemnification as a social function. For us, to compare the liability of the criminal to repair the loss caused by his crime with the liability arising from breach of contract is simply immoral.

Crime, just as it implies a social reaction in the form of an indefinite segregation of the criminal, when the act is serious and the author dangerous, ought also to imply a social reaction in the shape of indemnification, accessory to segregation when that is necessary, or adequate by itself for social defence when the act is not serious, and the author is not dangerous. For slight offences by occasional criminals, strict indemnification will, on the one hand, avoid the disadvantages of short terms of imprisonment, and will, on the other hand, be much more efficacious and sensible than an assured provision of food and shelter, for a few days or weeks, in the State prisons.

Indemnification may naturally take two forms, as a fine or an indemnity payable to the State, and as an indemnity or a reparation payable to the injured person.

It may also be added that the State should be made responsible for the rights of the victims, and give them immediate satisfaction, especially for crimes of violence, recouping itself from the offender, as it does, or ought to do, for legal costs.

The evolution of punishment is a striking proof of this. First, the reaction against crime is an entirely private concern; then it assumes a weaker form in pecuniary reparation, whereof, by and by, a portion goes to the State, which presently retains the whole sum, leaving to the victim the poor consolation of proceeding separately for an indemnification. Nothing therefore could be more in accord with this evolution of punishment than the proposed reform, whereby the indemnification of a merely private injury, as it is regarded in the primitive phase of penal justice, becomes a public function, so far as it is the legal and social consequence of the offence.

The classical principles in this respect, and the practical consequences which flow from them, are more like a humorous farce than an institution of justice; and it is only the force of habit which prevents the world from realising its full comicality.

In fine, citizens pay taxes in return for the public services of the State, amongst which that of public security is the chief. And the State actually expends millions every year upon this social function. Nevertheless, every crime which is committed is followed by a grotesque comedy. The State, which is responsible for not having been able to prevent crime, and to give a better guarantee to the citizens, arrests the criminal (if it can arrest him--and seventy per cent. of DISCOVERED crimes go unpunished). Then, with the accused person before it, the State, ``which ought to concern itself with the lofty interests of eternal justice,'' does not concern itself with the victims of the crime, leaving the indemnification to their prosaic ``private interest,'' and to a separate invocation of justice. And then the State, in the name of eternal justice, exacts from the criminal, in the shape of a fine payable into the public treasury, a compensation for its own defence--which it does not secure, even when the crime is only a trespass upon private property!

Thus the State, which cannot prevent crime, and can only repress it in a small number of cases, and which fails accordingly in its first duty, for which the citizens pay it their taxes, demands a price for all this! And then again the State, sentencing a million and a half to imprisonment within ten years, puts the cost of food and lodging on the shoulders of the same citizens, whom it has failed either to defend or to indemnify for the loss which they have suffered! And all in the name of eternal retributive justice.

This method of ``administering justice" must be radically altered. The State must indemnify individuals for the damage caused by crimes which it has not been able to prevent (as is partially recognised in cases of public disaster), recouping itself from the criminals.

Only then shall we secure a strict reparation of damage, for the State will put in motion its inexorable fiscal machinery, as it now does for the recovery of taxes; and on the other hand the principle of social community of interests will be really admitted and applied, not only against the individual but also for him. For we believe that if the individual ought to be always responsible for the crimes which he commits, he ought also to be always indemnified for the crimes of which he is the victim.

In any case, as the indefinite segregation of the criminal is the fundamental principle of the positive system of social defence against crime, apart from the technical systems of imprisonment and detention, so indemnification as a social function is a second essential principle, apart from the special rules of procedure for carrying it into effect.

These two fundamental principles of the positive system would still be incomplete if they did not come into practical operation according to a general rule, which leads up to the practical organisation of social defence--that is to say, the adaptation of defensive measures to the various criminal types.

The tendency of the classical theories on crime and prison discipline is in sharp contrast, for their ideal is the ``uniformity of punishment" which lies at the base of all the more recent penal codes.

If for the classical school the criminal is but an average and abstract type, the whole difference of treatment is, of course, reduced to a graduation of the ``amount of crime" and the ``amount of punishment." And then it is natural that this punitive dosing should be more difficult when the punishments are different in kind, and not very similar in their degrees of coincident afflictive and correctional power. Thus the ideal becomes a single punishment, apportioned first by the legislature and then by the judge, in an indefinite number of doses.

Here and there a solitary voice has been heard, even amongst the classical experts, objecting to this tendency towards dogmatic uniformity; but it has had no influence. The question brought forward by M. D'Alinge at the Prison Congress in London (Proceedings, 1872, p. 327), ``whether the moral classification of prisoners ought to be the main foundation of penitentiary systems, either in association or on the cellular plan," which he himself decided in the affirmative, was not so much as discussed, and it was not even referred to at the successive Congresses at Stockholm (1878), Rome (1885), and St. Petersburg (1889). On the contrary, the Congress at Stockholm decided that, ``reserving minor and special punishments for certain slight infractions of the law, or for such as do not point to the corrupt nature of their authors, it is desirable to adopt for every prison system the greatest possible legal assimilation of punishments by imprisonment, with no difference except in their duration, and the consequences following upon release."[20]

[20] Proceedings, i. 138-70, 551-7, 561-3. Now and then, however, a prison expert of more positive tendencies maintains ``the very great use, or rather the scientific necessity, of the classification of prisoners as a basis for the punitive and prison system" (Beltrani Scalia.)

To positivists, the ``uniformity of punishment," even of mere detention, appears simply absurd, since it ignores the capital fact of different categories of criminals.

There must be homogeneity between the evil and its remedy; for, as Dumesnil says, ``the prisoner is a moral (I would add a physical) patient, more or less curable, and we must apply to him the great principles of the art of medicine. To a diversity of ills we must apply a diversity of remedies."

In this connection, however, we must avoid the two extremes, uniformity of punishment and the so-called individualisation of punishment, the latter especially in fashion amongst American prison experts. No doubt it would be a desirable thing to apply a particular treatment to each convict, after a physical and psychological study of his individuality, and of the conditions which led him into crime; but this is not practicable when the number of prisoners is very great, and the managing staff have no adequate notions of criminal biology and psychology. How can a governor individualise the penal treatment of four or five hundred prisoners? And does not the cellular system, which reduces the characteristic manifestations of the personal dispositions of prisoners to a minimum, levelling them all by the uniformity of routine and silence, render it impossible to observe and get to know the special character of each condemned person, and so specialising the discipline? Where, too, are we to find the necessary governors and warders who would know how to discharge this difficult duty? The solid fact that particular houses of correction or punishment are in excellent condition when their governors have the psychological intuition of a De Metz, a Crofton, a Spagliardi, or a Roukawichnikoff, and languish when he departs, strikingly demonstrates that the whole secret of success lies in the spirit of a wise governor, skilled in psychology, rather than in the slender virtue of the cell.

Just as an imperfect code with good judges succeeds better than a ``monumental" code with foolish judges, so a prison system, however ingenious and symmetrical, is worthless without a staff to correspond.

And as the question of the staff is always very serious, especially for financial reasons, I believe that, instead of the impracticable idea of individualisation in punishment, we ought to substitute that of classification, which is equally efficacious and more easily applied. It cannot be denied that criminal anthropologists are not all agreed on the classification of criminals. But I have already shown that the differences between proposed classifications are only formal and of secondary importance; and again, the number of those who agree to the classification which I have proposed increases day by day.

Before inquiring how we can practically organise the positive system of social defence on the basis of this anthropological classification of criminals, we must bear in mind two rules, common to all the technical proposals of the same system.

First, care must be taken that segregation does not become or continue to be (as it is too often at present) a welcome refuge of idleness and criminal association, instead of a deprivation.

Penitentiaries for condemned prisoners--the classical prison experts make no distinction between their cells for prisoners before trial and those for convicts!-- should not be so comfortable as to excite the envy (a vast injustice and imprudence) of the honest and ill-fed rural labourer vegetating in his cottage, or of the working- man pining in his garret.

Secondly, the obligation to labour should be imperative for all who are in prison, except in case of sickness. Prisoners should pay the State, not as now for their tobacco and wine, but for food, clothes, and lodging, whilst the remainder of their earnings should go to indemnify their victims.

The classical theory declares that ``the State,'' as Pessina writes, ``being compelled to adopt deprivation of liberty as the principal means of penal repression and retribution, contracts an absolute obligation to provide those whom they punish in this way not only with bodily sustenance, but also with the means of supplying their intellectual and moral needs.'' So the State maintains in idleness the majority even of those who are said to be ``sentenced to hard labour,'' and the offence, after it has served the turn of the offender, further assures him free lodging and food, shifting the burden on to honest citizens.

I cannot see by what moral or legal right the crime ought to exempt the criminal from the daily necessity of providing for his own subsistence, which he experienced before he committed the crime, and which all honest men undergo with so many sacrifices. The irony of these consequences of the classical theories could not, in fact, be more remarkable. So long as a man remains honest, in spite of pathetic misery and sorrow, the State takes no trouble to guarantee for him the means of existence by his labour. It even bans those who have the audacity to remind society that every man, by the mere fact of living, has the right to live, and that, as work is the only means of obtaining a livelihood, every man has the right (as all should recognise the duty) of working in order to live.

But as soon as any one commits a crime, the State considers it its duty to take the utmost care of him, ensuring for him comfortable lodging, plenty of food, and light labour, if it does not grant him a happy idleness! And all this, again, in the name of eternal and retributive justice.

It may be added that our proposals are the only way of settling the oft-recurring question as to the economic competition (by the price of commodities), and the moral competition (in the regularity of work) which prison labour unjustly wages with free and honest labour. As a matter of fact, as prisoners can only remain idle or work, they must clearly be made to work. But they must be made to work at trades which come less into competition with free labour and it is especially necessary to give prisoners wages equal to those of free labourers, on condition that they pay the State for their food, clothes, and lodging, whilst the remainder goes to indemnify their victims.

Over the prison gates I should like to carve that maxim of universal application: "He who will not work, neither shall he eat."

V.

Since the novel proposals put forward half a century ago, amongst others by doctors Georget and Brierre de Boismont, a whole library of volumes has been published in favour of criminal lunatic asylums. A few voices here and there were heard in opposition or reserve, but these have almost entirely ceased.

Criminal lunatic asylums were adopted in England as early as 1786. In 1815 Bethlehem Hospital was appropriated to criminal lunatics, and the Broadmoor Asylum was founded in 1863. Similar asylums exist at Dundrum in Ireland (1850), at Perth in Scotland (1858), at New York (1874), and in Canada (1877).

On the continent of Europe there is not to this day a regular asylum for mad criminals, though France, after an experiment in treating condemned madmen at Bicetre, opened a separate wing for them in the prison at Gaillon. Holland has assigned to them the hospital of Bosmalen (Brabant); Germany has special wards in the establishments at Waldheim, Bruchsaal, Halle, and Hamburg; and Italy, after founding a special ward in 1876, at the establishment for relapsed prisoners at Aversa, has converted the Ambrogiana establishment at Montelupo in Tuscany, into an asylum for insane convicts, and for prisoners under observation as being of unsound mind. The new Italian penal code, though not openly recognising the foundation of asylums for criminals acquitted on the ground of insanity, has, in its

131

general spirit of eclecticism, given judges the power of handing them over to the competent authority when it would be dangerous to release them (Art. 46). At the Montelupo Asylum criminals acquitted on the ground of insanity are also detained, at first under observation, then by a definite order from the president of the Tribunal, who can revoke his order on the petition of the family, or of the authorities.

The inquiry into existing legislation on insane criminals, undertaken by the ``Societe Generale des prisons de Paris,'' showed that in France, Germany, Austria-Hungary, Croatia, Belgium, Portugal, and Sweden, the authors of crimes or offences who are acquitted on the ground of insanity are withdrawn from all control by the judicial authority, and entrusted to the more or less regular and effectual control of the administrative authority. In England, Holland, Denmark, Spain, and Russia, on the contrary, the judicial authority is empowered and even compelled to order the seclusion of these individuals in an ordinary or a criminal lunatic asylum.

Of the objections raised against this form of social defence against insane criminals, I pass over that of the cost, which is considerable; for even from the financial point of view I believe that the actual system, which gives no guarantee of security against madmen with criminal tendencies, is more costly to the administration, if only by reason of the damage which they cause. I also pass over the other objection, based on the violent scenes which are said to be inseparable from the association of such prisoners; for experience has shown that forebodings are ill founded in regard to criminal asylums where the inmates are classified according to their tendencies, under the direction of a staff with special knowledge, who are able to prevent such outbreaks. In ordinary asylums, on the other hand, a few insane criminals are sufficient to render the maintenance of order very difficult, and their inevitable and frequent outbreaks have dire effects on the other patients.

The most serious and repeated difficulties in regard to lunatic asylums spring from the very principles of the defensive function of society.

It is said in the first place that the author of a dangerous action is either a madman or else a criminal. If he is a madman, he has nothing to do with penal justice--so Fabret, Mendel, and others have said; his action is not a crime, for he had no control over himself, and he ought to go to an ordinary asylum, special measures being taken for him, as for every other dangerous madman. Or else he is a criminal, and then he has nothing to do with a lunatic asylum, and he ought to go to prison.

But there is a fallacy in this dilemma, for it leaves out the intermediate cases and types, where particular individuals are at the same time mad and criminal. And even if it were a question of madmen only, the logical consequence would not be to bar out special asylums, for it seems clear that if ordinary madmen (not criminals, that is, not the authors of dangerous actions) ought to go to an ordinary asylum, criminal madmen, or madmen with a tendency to commit dangerous or criminal actions, as

132

well as those who have committed them, ought to go to a special asylum for this category of madmen. For, on the other hand, we constantly see that administrative authorities which observe the same rules for the seclusion of ordinary and criminal madmen do not prevent the release of the latter, some time after the crime, when the disturbance of mind and even the recollection of the deed are all but effaced; and criminal madmen commit other violent or outrageous excesses, very soon after they are left exposed to their diseased tendencies.[21]

[21] M. Lunier, writing in 1881 of epileptics, and the method of treatment and aid appropriate to them, says that of 33,000 known epileptics in France, 5,200 only are in private or public asylums, whilst 28,000 remain with their families. From these figures it would appear very probable that these 28,000 epileptics left at liberty commit crimes and offences.

It may be answered that it is sufficient to have special wings in ordinary asylums, which would also get over the repugnance of families against the association of their quiet and harmless patients with murderous and outrageous madmen. But experience has already proved that these special wards do not work well, for it is too difficult with the same staff to apply such varied treatment and discipline as are necessary for ordinary and criminal lunatics.

Fabret says that "a so-called criminal, when he is seen to be mad, should cease to be regarded as a criminal, and ought purely and simply to resume his ordinary rights."

But, in the first place, if a madman is distinguished from all other inoffensive madmen by the grave fact of having killed, or burned, or outraged, it is clear that he cannot "purely and simply" return to the same kind of treatment which is given to harmless lunatics.

The truth is that this argument applies to a large number of ideas which science is continually weeding out, and which have proceeded on the assumption that madness is an involuntary misfortune which must be treated, and that crime is a voluntary fault which must be chastised. It is evident on the other hand that crime as well as folly, being the result of abnormal conditions of the individual, and of the physical and social environment, is always a question for social defence, whether it is or is not accompanied in the criminal by a more or less manifest and clinical form of mental malady.

The same reply holds good for the second objection to asylums for criminal madmen, when it is said that a madman cannot, for the sole reason that he has killed or stolen, be shut up indefinitely, perhaps for ever, in an asylum.

Mancini, who was keeper of the seals, and at the same time a great criminal pleader, aptly expressed the ideas of the classical school when replying to an interpellation of Deputy Righi on the foundation of criminal lunatic asylums:--``I could never understand how the same court, which is obliged by law to acquit upon a verdict of the jury that the accused is insane, and therefore not responsible, could also decree the compulsory seclusion in an asylum, for any period, of the same accused person. . . . Is it because he has committed a crime? But that is not true, for the man who did not know what he was doing, and who for that reason has been declared innocent before the law, and irresponsible, cannot have committed a crime. There is consequently no legal reason why he should lose the exercise and enjoyment of that liberty which is not denied to any other unfortunate beings who are diseased like himself."

It would be impossible to put more clearly the pure classical theory on crime and punishment; but perhaps it would be equally impossible to show less solicitude for social defence against criminal attacks. For it is certain that the mad murderer ``has committed no crime" from the ethical and legal point of view of the classical school; but it is still more certain that there is a dead man, and a family left behind who may be ruined by the deed, and it is very probable that this homicide, ``innocent before the law," will renew his outrage on other victims--and at any rate they are innocent.

And as for the indefinite period of seclusion in an asylum, it is well to remember, from the point of view of individual rights, that the formula with which a mad criminal is committed to an asylum ``during her Majesty's pleasure" had its origin in England, in the classic land of the habeas corpus--the sheet anchor of the ordinary citizen. Again, it is easy to see that the indefinite seclusion of mad criminals is rendered necessary by the same reasons which create the fundamental rule for criminals of every kind. It may therefore come to a question of allowing or disallowing the general principles of the positive school. But it cannot be denied that they are unassailable, both in theory and in practice. Crime is a phenomenon as natural as madness--the existence of society compels the organised community to defend itself against every anti-social action of the individual--the only difficulty is to adapt the form and duration of this self- defence to the form and intensity (the motives, conditions, and consequences) of the action. Indefinite seclusion, therefore, in a special establishment is inevitable on account of the special condition of these individuals.

The practical considerations of social defence are so strong that the great majority of classical criminal experts now accept criminal lunatic asylums, in spite of their manifest contradiction of the formal theories of moral responsibility, on the strength of which these asylums were, and still are, opposed by the intransigents of the classical school. This is why the new Italian penal code, in spite of its progressive aim, had not the courage in 1889 to adopt them frankly; and in the definitive text, as in the ministerial draft, it took refuge in an eclectic arrangement which has already met with a crowd of obstacles, due to the vagueness of the principles inspiring the code.

These criminal lunatic asylums ought to be of two kinds, differing in their discipline, one for the insane authors of serious and dangerous crimes, such as homicide, incendiarism, rape, and the like; and the other for slighter crimes, such as petty theft, violent language, outrages on public decency, and the like. For the latter, seclusion should be shorter than for the others. Thus in England convicts are sent to the State Asylum at Broadmoor, whilst minor offenders are sent to a county asylum.

Persons thus confined should be (1) prisoners acquitted on the ground of insanity, or sentenced for a fixed period, at the preliminary inquiry; (2) convicts who become insane during the expiation of their sentence; (3) insane persons who commit crimes in the ordinary asylums; (4) persons under observation for weak intellect in special wards, who have been put on their trial, and given grounds for suspecting madness.

At Broadmoor, on December 31, 1867, there were 389 male patients and 126 female; and in 1883 there were 381 males and 132 females, thus classified:--

Mad Criminals. Male. Female.

Murder ... ... 155 ... 85 Attempted murder... ... ... 111 ... 18 Parricide... ... ... 7 ... 6 Theft ... ... 23 ... 3

Mad Criminals. Male. Female.

Incendiarism ... ... 24 ... 1 Military offence ... ... 21 ... -- Attempted suicide... ... ... 3 ... {?}

In Germany, in the prison at Waldheim, the proportion of mad criminals to the corresponding classes of ordinary criminals was as follows:--

Percentage
Crimes. In Prison. Insane.

Homicide, actual or attempted ... 74 ... 17.6 Murder and malicious wounding ... 51 ... 9.8 Highway robbery with violence ... 64 ... 12.5 Incendiarism ... ... 219 ... 6.8 Rape ... ... 52 ... 5.8 Indecent assault ... ... 299 ... 5.7 Perjury ... ... 220 ... 2.7 Military crimes ... ... 23 ... 21.7 Crimes against property ... ... 5,116 ... 1.9 Other offences ... ... 158 ... 0.6

---- ----

Total ... ... 6,276 ... 2.7

135

That is to say, there was (1) a very large proportion of madmen amongst the military offenders, which may point to the effect of military life, or else a careless selection for conscription, or both causes taken together; and (2) a greater proportion of mad criminals amongst the more serious offenders, partly because the authors of crimes of violence are subjected to more strict and frequent observation for madness.

It seems to me that this fact, which is also confirmed by the figures for England, is the most cogent argument in favour of criminal lunatic asylums.

For born criminals, since, as Dr. Maudsley says, we are face to face, if not exactly with a degenerate species, at least with a degenerate variety of the human species, and the problem is to diminish their number as much as possible, a preliminary question at once arises, namely, whether the penalty of death is not the most suitable and efficacious form of social defence against the anti-social class, when they commit crimes of great gravity.

It is a question which for a century past has divided the criminal experts and wearied the general public, with perhaps more sentimental declamations than positive contributions; a question revived by the positive school, which, however, only brought it forward, without discussing it, at the first Congress on Criminal Anthropology at Rome; whilst it has been recently settled by the new Italian penal code, which is the first code amongst the leading States to decree (January 1, 1890) the legal abolition of the death penalty, after its virtual abolition in Italy since the year 1876, except for military crimes.

Amongst the classical experts, as amongst the positivists, there are those who would abolish and those who would retain the death penalty; but the disagreement on this subject is not equally serious in the two camps. For whilst the classical abolitionists almost all assert that the death penalty is inequitable, the positivists are unanimous in declaring it legitimate, and only a few contest its practical efficacy.

It seems to me that the death penalty is prescribed by nature, and operates at every moment in the life of the universe. Nor is it opposed to justice, for when the death of another man is absolutely necessary it is legitimate, as in the cases of lawful self-defence, whether of the individual or of society, which is admitted by classical abolitionists such as Beccaria and Carrara.

The universal law of evolution shows us also that vital progress of every kind is due to continual selection, by the death of the least fit in the struggle for life. Now this selection, in humanity as with the lower animals, may be natural or artificial. It would therefore be in agreement with natural laws that human society should make an artificial selection, by the elimination of anti-social and incongruous individuals.

We ought not, however, to carry these conclusions too far, for every problem has its relative bearings, and positive observation, unlike logic, does not admit simple and exact solutions. It must be observed that this idea of artificial selection, though true, would lead to exaggerated conclusions, if it were carried into the sociological field without reserve, and without the necessary balance between the interests and rights of the community and of individuals. If this idea were taken absolutely, indeed, it would render legitimate and even obligatory an ultra-Spartan elimination of all children born abortive or incurably diseased, or anti- social through their idiotcy or mental insanity.

On the other hand, to recognise that the death penalty may be legitimate as an extreme and exceptional measure is not to acknowledge that it is necessary in the normal conditions of social life. Now it cannot be questioned that in these normal conditions society may defend itself otherwise than by death, as by perpetual seclusion or transportation, the failure of which, by the escape of convicts, is too rare to be decisive against it.

The preventive and deterrent efficacy of the death penalty is very problematical when we examine it not by our own impressions as average human beings, calmly and theoretically, but with the data of criminal psychology, which is its only true sphere of observation. Every one who commits a crime is either carried away by sudden passion, when he thinks of nothing, or else he acts coolly and with premeditation, and then he is determined in his action, not by a dubious comparison between the death penalty and imprisonment for life, but simply by a hope of impunity. This is especially the case with born criminals, whose main psychological characteristic is an excess of improvidence, combined with moral insensibility.

If a convict tells us that he fears death, this merely means that he has the momentary impression, which cannot, however, restrain him from crime, for here again, by the same psychological tendency, he will be subject only to the criminal temptation.

And if it is true that, when the criminal has been tried and condemned, he fears death more than imprisonment for life (always excepting condemned suicides, and those who by their physical and moral insensibility laugh at death up to the foot of the scaffold), it is none the less necessary to try and to condemn them.

Indeed statistics prove that the periodic variations of the more serious crimes is independent of the number of condemnations and executions, for they are determined by very different causes. Tuscany, where there has been no death penalty for a century, is one of the provinces with the lowest number of serious crimes; and in France, in spite of the increase of general crime and of population, charges of murder, poisoning, parricide, and homicide, dropped from 560 in 1826 to 430 in 1888, though the number of executions diminished in the same period from 197 to 9.

137

The death penalty is an easy panacea, but it is far from being capable of solving a problem so complex as that of serious crime. The idea of killing off the incorrigibles and the born criminals is easily conceived, and Diderot, in his Letter to Landois, maintained that it was a natural consequence of the denial of free-will, saying: ``What is the grand distinction between man and man? Doing good and doing harm. The man who does harm ought to be extinguished, not punished." But as against this too facile notion we must look to experience, and to the other material and moral conditions of social life, for the necessary balance and completion.

I will not further discuss the death penalty, for it is by this time an exhausted question from the intellectual standpoint, and has passed into the domain of prejudice for or against, and this prejudice is concerned rather with the more or less repugnant method of execution than with the penalty itself. In its favour there is the absolute, irrevocable, and instantaneous elimination from society of an individual who has shown himself absolutely unadaptable, and dangerous to society. But I hold that, if we would draw from the death penalty the only positive utility which it possesses, namely, artificial selection, then we must have courage enough to apply it resolutely in all cases where it is necessary from this point of view, that is to say, to all born criminals, who are the authors of the most serious crimes of violence. In Italy, for example, it would be necessary to execute at least one thousand persons every year, and in France nearly two hundred and fifty, in place of the annual seven or eight.

Otherwise the death penalty must be considered as an unserviceable and neglected means of terror, merely to be printed in the codes; and in that case it would be acting more seriously to abolish it.

So regarded it is too much like those motionless scarecrows which husbandmen set up in their fields, dotted about with the foolish notion that the birds will be frightened away from the corn. They may cause a little alarm at first sight; but by and by the birds, seeing that the scarecrow never moves and cannot hurt them, lose their fear, and even perch on the top of it. So it is with criminals when they see that the death penalty is never or very rarely applied; and one cannot doubt that criminals judge of the law, not by its formulation in the codes, but by its practical and daily application.

Since the deterrent efficacy of punishments in general, including the death penalty, is quite insignificant for the born criminals, who are insensible and improvident, the rare cases of execution will certainly not cure the disease of society. Only the slaughter of several hundred murderers every year would have a sensible result in the way of artificial selection; but that is more easily said than done. And I imagine that, at normal periods, in no modern and civilised State would a series of daily executions of the capital sentence be possible. Public opinion would not endure it, and a reaction would soon set in.[22]

[22] In every case I think that executions should take place in prison, and by means of a poison administered as soon as the sentence takes effect. In North America electricity has been tried, but executions by this process appear to be as horrible and repulsive as those by the guillotine, the garotte, the scaffold, or the rifle. (See the Medico-Legal Journal of New York, March and September, 1889.) From the ``Summarised Information on Capital Punishment," published by the Howard Association in 1881, I take the following figures on capital punishment in Europe and America:--

Death
State. Sentences. Executions.

Austria (1870-9) ... ... 806 ... 16 France (1870-9) ... ... 198 ... 93 Spain (1868-77) ... ... 291 ... 26 Sweden (1869-78) ... ... 32 ... 3 Denmark (1868-77) ... ... 94 ... 1 Bavaria (1870-9) ... ... 240 ... 7 Italy (1867-76) ... ... 392 ... 34 Germany, North (1869-78) ... ... 484 ... 1 England (1860 79)... ... ... 665 ... 372 Ireland (1860-79) ... ... 66 ... 36 Scotland (1860-79 ... ... 40 ... 15 Australia and New Zealand (1870-9... 453 ... 123 United States, about 2,500 murders annually--about 100 executions and 100 lynchings annually.

In Finland, between 1824 and 1880 there was no execution. In Holland, Portugal, Roumania, and Italy, capital punishment is abolished by law; and in Belgium virtually. Switzerland also has abolished it, but a few cantons, under the influence of a few atrocious and recurrent crimes, revived it in their codes, but did not carry it out. In the United States it has been abolished in Michigan, Wisconsin, Rhode Island, and Maine. An inquiry into the legislation and statistics relating to murder in Europe and America was instituted by Lord Granville in July, 1880 and the results were published in 1881. (``Reports on the Laws of Foreign Countries respecting Homicidal Crime.")

In a manuscript register of executions in the Duchy of Ferrara between 970 and 1870, I found that, excluding the nineteenth century, there were 5,627 executions in 800 years (3,981 for theft, and 1,009 for homicide), that is an average of 700 in each century, in the city of Ferrara alone. And at Rome, according to the records of the Convent of St. John the Beheaded, between 1500 and 1770 there were 5,280 executions, or 1,955 in each century, in the city of Rome alone. Now, if we consider the proportion of population in Ferrara and Rome to that of Italy as a whole, we reach an enormous number of executions in former centuries, which can scarcely have been fewer than four hundred every year.

These were serious applications of the death penalty, to which we certainly owe in some degree the purification of society by the elimination of individuals who would otherwise have swelled their criminal posterity.

139

In conclusion, if we wish to treat the death penalty seriously, and derive from it the only service of which it is capable, we must apply it on this enormous scale; or else, if it is retained as an ineffectual terror, we should be acting more seriously if we were to expunge it from the penal code, after excluding it from our ordinary practice. And as I shall certainly not have the courage to ask for the restoration of these mediaeval modes of extermination, I am still, for the practical considerations above mentioned, a convinced abolitionist, especially for such countries as Italy, where a more or less artificial and superficial current of public opinion is keenly opposed to capital punishment.

Setting aside the death penalty, as unnecessary in normal times, and inapplicable in the only proportions which would make it efficacious, for the born criminals who commit the most serious crimes, there remains only a choice between these two modes of elimination--transportation for life and indefinite seclusion.

This is the only choice for the positivists; for we cannot attach much importance to the opinion of the German jurists, Holtzendorff, Geyer, and others, who would do away with perpetual imprisonment altogether. Professor Lucchini took up this theory in Italy, saying that the personal freedom of the convict ought to be limited in its exercise, but not suppressed as a right, and that imprisonment for life destroys ``the moral and legal personality of the criminal in one of its most important human factors, the sociable instinct.'' He added that punishment ``ought not to become exhausted by excess of duration.''

Surely it is not speaking seriously to say that the right of the individual cannot be suppressed if necessity demands it, when we see it done every day in cases of legitimate self-defence; and that punishment is exhausted by excess of duration, when it is precisely the duration of banishment from one's kind which constitutes the only real efficacy of punishment; and to speak of the sociable instinct in connection with the most anti-social criminals.

And it is only by oblivion of the elementary and least contestable data of criminal bio-psychology that the exclusion of all life- punishments can be maintained, on the ground that this perpetuity ``is contrary to the reformative principle of punishment, to the principle that punishment ought to aim not only at afflicting the prisoner, but also at arousing in him, if possible, the moral sense, or at strengthening him, and opening up to him a path by which he can hope to be readmitted into society, amended and rehabilitated. Perpetuity of punishment excludes this possibility.''

The framers of the Dutch penal code replied to these observations of Professor Pols, first in the name of common sense, that ``punishment is not inflicted for the benefit of the prisoner, but for that of society,'' and secondly, with something of irony, that ``even for the sake of the abolition of capital punishment, and to prevent a reaction in favour of this punishment, we must uphold the right of shutting up for ever the few malefactors whose release would be dangerous."

It is entirely futile to consider the amendment of criminals as opposed to imprisonment for life, when it is known that born criminals, authors of the most serious crimes, for whom such punishment is reserved, are precisely those whose amendment is impossible, and that the moral sense attributed to them is only a psychological fallacy of the classical psychologist, who attributes to the conscience of the criminal that which he feels in his own honest and normal conscience.

But it is easy enough to see that this opposition to perpetual detention, though it has remained without effect, as being too doctrinaire and sentimental, is only a symptom of the historical tendency of the classical schools, entirely in favour of the criminal, and always tending to the relaxation of punishments. The interests of society are too much disregarded when it is sought to pass from the abolition of capital punishment to that of imprisonment for life. If the tendency is not checked, we may expect to see some classical expert demanding the abolition of all punishment for these unfortunate criminals, with their delicate moral sensibilities!

The question, therefore, is between transportation or indefinite seclusion.

Much has been written for and against transportation, and there was a lively discussion of the problem in Italy, some twenty years ago, between M. Beltrani Scalia, a former director-general of prisons, and the advocates of this form of elimination of criminals. Without going into the details of the controversy, it is evident that the experience of countries like England, which for a long time transported its criminals at a cost of hundreds of millions, and then abandoned the practice, is in itself a noteworthy example.

Yet it is only an objection, so far as it goes, against transportation as formerly practised, that is to say, with enormous prisons built in distant lands. M. Beltrani Scalia justly said that we might as well build them at home, for they will cost less and be more serviceable. The example of France in its practical application of this policy is not encouraging.

However, there is in transportation, as in the death penalty, an unquestionable element of reason. For when it is perpetual, with very faint chances of return, it is the best mode of ridding society of its most injurious factors, without our being compelled to keep them in those compulsory human hives which are known as cellular prisons.

But again, there is the question of simple transportation, first put into practice by England, which consists of planting convicts on an island or desert continent, with the opportunity of living by labour, or else of letting them loose in a savage country, where the convicts, who in civilised countries are themselves half savage, would represent a partial civilisation, and, from being highwaymen and murderers, might become military leaders in countries where, at any rate, the revival of their criminal tendencies would meet with an immediate and energetic resistance, in place of the slow machinery of our criminal trials.

For Italy, however, the question presents itself in a special form; for there a sort of internal deportation, in the lands which are not tilled on account of the malaria, would be far more serviceable. If the dispersion of this malaria demands a human hecatomb, it would evidently be better to sacrifice criminals than honest husbandmen. Transportation across the sea was very difficult for Italy a few years ago, especially in view of the lack of colonies; for then there was always the obstacle of which Franklin spoke in reference to transported English convicts, in his well-known retort: "What would you say if we were to transport our rattlesnakes to England?" But since Italy has had her colony of Erythrea the idea of transportation has been taken up again. In May, 1890, I brought forward a resolution in Parliament in favour of an experimental penal colony in our African dependencies. The proposal found many supporters, in spite of the opposition of the keeper of the seals, who forgot that he had written in his report on the draft penal code that prisoners might also be detained in the colonies. Soon afterwards the proposal was renewed by Deputy De Zerbi, and accepted by M. Beltrani Scalia, director-general of prisons.

In a similar manner M. Prins declares himself in favour of transportation for Belgium, since the constitution of the Congo State.

But it is my matured opinion that transportation ought not to be an end in itself. The penal colony for adults ought to be a pioneer of the free agricultural colony. The problem of a penal colony in our African possessions cannot, therefore, be solved in advance of two other questions.

Before all, we must see whether these possessions offer suitable districts for agricultural colonisation. And secondly, we must consider whether convicts would not cost less to transport into districts nearer home which need to be cleared, a plan which would also prevent their going over to the enemy, becoming leaders or guides of the barbarous tribes which are at war with us.

In any case, whether we decide on transportation to the interior or beyond the seas, for born and habitual criminals, there is still the question as to the form of seclusion.

In this connection the idea has been suggested of "establishments for incorrigibles," or hardened criminals, wherein should be confined for life, or (the same thing in this case) for an indefinite period, born criminals who have committed serious crimes, habitual criminals, and confirmed recidivists.

The congenital character and hereditary transmission of criminal tendencies in these individuals fully justify the words of Quetelet, that "moral diseases are like physical diseases: they are contagious, or epidemic, or hereditary. Vice is transmitted in some families in the same way as scrofula or consumption. The greater number of crimes come from a comparatively few families, which need a special supervision, an isolation like that which we impose on sick persons suspected of carrying the germs of infection." So Aristotle speaks of a man who, being accused of beating his father, answered: "My father beat my grandfather, who used to beat his father cruelly; and you see my son--before he is grown up he will fly into passions and beat me." And Plutarch added to this: "The sons of vicious and corrupt men reproduce the very nature of their parents."

This is the explanation of Plato's idea, who, "admitting the principle that children ought not to suffer for the crimes of their parents, yet, putting the case of a father, a grandfather, and a great-grandfather who had been condemned to death, proposed that their descendants should be banished, as belonging to an incorrigible family." Carrara called this a mistaken idea, but it seems to us to be substantially just. It may be remembered that when De Metz in 1839 founded his agricultural penal colony at Metray, once celebrated but now in decay (for the whole success of these foundations depends on the exceptional psychological qualities of their governors), out of 4,454 children, 871, or 20 per cent., were the children of convicts. We quite agree with Crofton's proposal to place the children of convicts in industrial schools or houses of correction.

A special establishment for the perpetual or indefinite seclusion of incorrigible criminals has been proposed or approved in Italy by Lombroso, Curcio, Barini, Doria, Tamassia, Garofalo, Carelli; in France by Despine, Labatiste, Tissot, Leveille; in Russia by Minzloff; in England by May; in Germany by Kraepelin and Lilienthal; in Austria by Wahlberg; in Switzerland by Guillaume; in America by Wines and Wayland; in Holland by Van Hamel; in Portugal by Lucas; &c.

But I believe that, in order to establish the fact of incorrigibility, the number of relapses should vary in regard to different criminals and crimes. Thus, for instance, in the case of murders, especially by born criminals, the first crime should lead to an order for imprisonment for life. In the case of less serious crimes, such as rape, theft, wounding, swindling, &c., from two to four relapses should be necessary before the habitual criminal is sentenced to such imprisonment.

These ideas are approximately carried out, especially in the countries which, having made no great advance in the criminal sciences, meet with less of pedantic opposition to practical reforms.

Thus we find that France, after the proposals of Michaux, Petit, and Migneret, and especially after the advocacy of M. Reinach, followed by several publications of a like kind, agreed to the law of 1885 on the treatment of recidivism.

Messrs. Murray Brown and Baker spoke at the Prison Congress at Stockholm and at the Societe Generale des Prisons at Paris, of the system of cumulative and progressive sentences adopted, though not universally, in England with respect to hardened criminals. The term of imprisonment is increased, almost regularly, on each new relapse. This is the system which had already been suggested by Field and Walton Pearson at the Social Science Congress in October, 1871, and subsequently by Cox and Call, who was head of the police at Glasgow, at the Congress of 1874, and which, as Mr. Movatt pointed out, was adopted in the Indian penal code, and had been established in Japan by a decree fixing perpetual imprisonment after the fourth relapse.

The delegate from Canada at the Prison Congress at Stockholm testified that short terms of imprisonment increased the number of offences. ``After a first sentence many offenders in this class become professional criminals. Professional thieves, who are habitual offenders, ought, with few exceptions, to be sentenced to imprisonment for life, or for a term equivalent to the probable remainder of their life." The draft Russian code, in 1883, provides that, ``If it is found that the accused is guilty of several offences, and that he has committed them through habitual criminality, or as a profession, the court, when deciding upon the punishment in relation to the different crimes, may increase it," &c. And the Italian penal code, though with much timidity, has decreed a special increase of punishment for prisoners ``who have relapsed several times."

Quite recently, Senator Berenger introduced a measure in France ``on the progressive increase of punishment in cases of relapse," which became law on March 26, 1891, under the title of ``the modification and increase of punishments."

It is therefore very probable that even the classical criminalists will end by accepting the indefinite seclusion of hardened criminals, as they have already come to accept criminal lunatic asylums, though both ideas are opposed to the classical theories.

This is so true that at the Prison Congress at St. Petersburg in 1889 the question was first propounded ``whether it can be admitted that certain criminals should be regarded as incorrigible, and, if so, what means could be employed to protect society against this class of convicts." And speaking as a delegate from the Law Society of St. Petersburg, M. Spasovitch acknowledged that ``this question bore the stamp of its origin on its face. Of all the questions in the programme, it seemed to be the only one directly inspired by the principles of the new positive school of criminal anthropology, whose theories, propagated beyond the land of their birth in Italy, tended to a radical reform in science as well as in legislation, in the penal law as well as in procedure, in ideas of crime as well as in the modes of repression."

The Congress, in spite of some expressions of reserve, as when Madame Arenal platonically observed that ``an uncorrected criminal is not synonymous with an incorrigible criminal,'' adopted the following resolution:--``Without admitting that from the penal and penitentiary point of view there are any absolutely incorrigible criminals''--which is pure pedantry--``yet since experience shows that there are in fact individuals who resist the combined action of punishment and imprisonment''-- a notable admission!--``and who habitually and almost professionally renew their violation of the laws of society, this section of the Congress is unanimously of opinion that it is necessary to adopt special measures against such individuals.''

Similarly the International Union of Penal Law, in its session at Berne (August, 1890), expressed the opinions of the majority in the following terms:--``There are malefactors for whom, in view of their physical and moral condition, the constant application of ordinary punishments is inadequate. In this class are specially included the hardened recidivists, who ought to be considered as degenerate criminals, or criminals by profession. Malefactors ought to be subjected, according to the degree of their degeneration, or of the danger which they threaten, to special measures, framed with the purpose of preventing them from inflicting harm, and of amending them if possible.'' And in the session at Christiania (August, 1891), after the remarkable contribution of Van Hamel, the Union, after rejecting the proposition of Felisch, which spoke of ``the uncorrected'' in place of the ``incorrigible,'' unanimously approved the conclusions of Van Hamel:--``With a view to the more complete study of the character and injurious influence of habitual offenders, notably of such as are incorrigible (a study which is absolutely indispensable for legislation), the Union instructs its officers to urge upon the various Governments the great importance of statistics of recidivism which shall be detailed, precise, uniform, and adapted for comparative study. For incorrigible habitual offenders it is absolutely necessary that the trial on the last charge shall not definitely determine the treatment of the offender, but that the decision shall be carried on to a further inquiry, which shall have regard to the offender personally, to his past, and to his conduct during a fixed period of observation.

It is now necessary to inquire what form the perpetual or indefinite segregation of the criminal should assume.

Two great innovations in regard to prisons, as M. Tarde observes, have been made or developed within the past century, which are not yet adopted in every country: penal colonies, whereof transportation is only a factor, and the prison cell. The cell has assumed a leading position since it was brought over from America to Europe, where, however, the cellular prisons of St. Michael at Rome, and of Gand, had preceded it.

145

The cellular system, a product of the reaction against the enormous physical and moral putrefaction of the inmates of common prisons and labour establishments, may have had, and doubtless still has many advocates, amongst other reasons for the spirit of pietism and religious penitence which always goes with it; but it is open to strong criticism.

There has already been, amongst the same prison experts, a certain retrogressive movement in regard to isolation. Absolute and continued isolation, indeed, both by day and by night (``solitary confinement'') was at first recommended, even to the introduction, grotesque in spite of good intentions, of hoods and masks for the prisoners, a mediaeval reminiscence almost parallel with the Brothers of Pity in some Italian towns, for help to the wounded. Presently it was seen that this sort of thing certainly could not assist in the amendment of the guilty, and then isolation was relaxed (still making it applicable both by day and by night) with visits to prisoners by the chaplain, governors, and representatives of vigilance and prisoners' aid societies. This is called ``separate confinement.'' After this it was recognised that the real need for isolation was at night, and then the Auburn system was arrived at: isolation in cells by night, with daily labour in common, with an obligation (which cannot be enforced) of silence. And finally, seeing that in spite of the threefold panacea of every prison system (isolation, work, and instruction, especially religious instruction) relapses still increased, it was understood that it might not be very useful to subject a man for months or years to the monastic life of Trappist brothers, in these monstrous human hives (which Bentham brought to the notice of the French Constituent Assembly under the name of ``panopticons''), and to discharge him from prison at the end of his term, and plunge him into all the temptations of an atmosphere to which his lungs had become disaccustomed.

Then the ``progressive system'' was introduced, first in England, where it was devised by Maconochie, next in Ireland, which has given it a name, alternated with that of Sir W. Crofton. This is the most symmetrically perfect machinery, though reminding one somewhat of a company of marionettes. It confirms what was said by Haeckel, that the actual is a summary of the moods of aspiration, for it precisely sums up the systems which preceded it, each of which constitutes a phase of the progressive system. There is first of all a period of brotherly charity--absolute isolation for the prisoner to fall back upon his conscience, or to listen to the voice of remorse, or to receive an impression of devotion and fear. After this comes the Auburnian phase, of isolation by night and labour (when labour is accorded) by day, with the constraint of silence. Then an intermediary period in the agricultural colony or labour-gang outside the prison, like a period of convalescence, to accustom the lungs to the keen air of liberty. This is the phase added by Sir W. Crofton to the English system. Lastly comes the period of conditional release (on ticket of leave), whereby the last portion of the punishment is remitted, and will count as expiated if during the time of liberation, and for a succeeding period, the convict does not commit another crime.

The progressive or retrogressive passage from one phase to another is made by a sort of automatic regulator, depending on the number of marks gained or lost by the prisoner through his good or bad behaviour, to which we know the moral or psychological value to be attached--a value purely negative.

This progressive, gradual, or Irish system has obtained a supremacy in Europe, so that even Belgium, the classic land of the cellular system, reconsidered the ideas which it had based on daily experience, and was the first continental country to introduce conditional sentences (in 1888), which are the fruit of short sentences and cellular punishments.

I do not deny that this progressive system is better than the others, though we must not forget that the almost miraculous effects of amendment and decrease of recidivism (which indeed are claimed for every new system, only to be disproved later on) were due in Ireland to the wholesale emigration of those conditionally released to North America--an emigration amounting to 46 per cent. of the prisoners released. Nor must we forget that this system, which requires a trained staff of officers, is less difficult to work in countries where, as in Ireland, there are only a few hundred prisoners; but it would be much more difficult in Italy or France, where the prisoners are numbered by tens of thousands. In these countries, accordingly, the system will not be practical unless the principle of classifying prisoners in biological and psychological categories is conjoined with it; for without this we shall not get rid of the impersonal system which is the vice of our present penal law, and under which, even in our prison administration, we treat the prisoner as a mere symbol, to which we can apply the three conventional rules of the cell, hard labour, and instruction.

But I am strongly opposed to, or accept simply as accessory (even for the seclusion of prisoners before trial, after the preliminary examination), cellular isolation by itself, which has reached the height of absurdity and inhumanity in cases of imprisonment for life.

As Mancini said in 1876, discussing the draft of the Italian penal code, ``the punishment of hard labour for life, which is substituted in the draft for the capital sentence, differs substantially in its severity of privation and misery from all other modes of imprisonment. It must be undergone in one or two special prisons to be erected within the country. It would be the saddest and most terrible thing which the imagination of man could conceive. These tombs of the living, whom society has rejected for ever, unlike all other prisons, will condemn their inmates to continuous solitary immurement in cells, and to a life which may be worse than death itself. . . . This most wretched condition, which the free man cannot realise without horror, is to last ten years; and it is not to be in the power of man to bring it to an end sooner, if the prisoner, broken down by physical weakness, or threatened by loss of reason, cannot endure it any longer."

After this description, I am not sorry that I denounced the cellular system as one of the madnesses of the nineteenth century.

This useless, stupid, inhuman, costly ``tomb of the living'' must be repudiated, even when reduced to its lowest terms by the new Italian code, wherein Parliament, accepting part of my amendment, fixes the term of absolute seclusion at seven years.

It will be seen by this description of cellular imprisonment that the classical criminal and prison experts have logically arrived at the conclusion that perpetual punishment should be abolished; and this renders recidivism possible even in murder. But it is clear that what we ought to abolish is not perpetual separation, but only the stupidly harsh form of isolation in cells--and this not only in life sentences, but in all sentences.

Cellular imprisonment is inhuman, because it blots out or weakens, in the cases of the least degenerate criminals, that social sense which was already feeble in them, and also because it inevitably leads to madness or consumption (by onanism, insufficient movement, air, &c.). Hence it drives the prison authorities, in order to avoid these disastrous consequences, to the injustice of building cells for murderers which are decidedly comfortable, and consequently a mockery of the honest wretchedness of the cottages and garrets of the poor. The treatment of mental diseases recognises a special form of insanity under the name of prison madness.

Cellular imprisonment, in temporary or indefinite sentences, can do nothing for the amendment of the guilty, especially because, when we do not amend the social environment, it is useless to lavish care on our prisoners if, as soon as they quit prison, they must return to the same conditions which led them into crime. No adequate social prevention can in any way be provided by the more or less arcadian devices of the prisoners' aid societies. The chief mistake of the prison experts has been to concentrate their attention exclusively on the cell and in the cell, forgetting the external factors of crime; so that, by a familiar psychological process, the cell has become for prison experts what money is to the avaricious: it has ceased to be a means, and has become an end in itself.

Again, the cellular system is ineffectual because the very isolation which was its original object is incapable of realisation. Prisoners find a thousand means of carrying on communication with each other, during their walks, or by writing on the leaves of books lent to them to read, or by knocking on their walls according to a conventional alphabet, or by writing in the sand, or by using the drains as telephonic receivers, as was done in the cellular prisons of Mazas, Milan, &c. Plain proofs of this may be found in Lombroso's ``Les Palimpsestes des Prisons.'' ``The public, and even well-informed persons, honestly believe that the cellular prison is a dumb and paralytic thing, without tongue or hands, simply because the law has ordered silence and inactivity. But as no decree, however vigorous, can counteract the nature of things, so this organism speaks, moves, occasionally wounds or slays, in spite of all the decrees. Only, as always happens when a necessity of humanity is opposed by a law, it acts by less known, underground and hidden means."

Moreover, the cellular system is unequal in its application, for difference of race has much to say to it, and in fact it is a clumsy machinery of the northern races, repugnant to those of the south, more dependent on the open air and light. Apart from that, isolation has very different effects amongst people of the same nation, according to the different vocations of the prisoners, especially of occasional offenders. In this connection the testimony of Faucher, Ferrus, and Tarde is thoroughly just, that in prison administration we ought to observe a distinction between dwellers in town and country.[23]

[23] Yet the question whether the cellular system should be modified in accordance with the nationality, social condition, and sex of criminals, which has not been brought forward since the Prison Congress at Stockholm, was there decided by the following resolution:--``The cellular system, where it is in operation, may be applied without distinction of race, social condition (as regards townsmen or rural population), or sex, provided that the authorities have regard to these special conditions in matters of detail. Exception may be made in respect of the young, and if cellular discipline is applied to them also, it should be in such a way as not to prejudice their physical and moral development." (``Proceedings," 1878, pp. 303, 617.)

Again, the cellular system is too costly to be adopted as the only form of imprisonment--which, however, is enacted in the Italian penal code, the French law of 1875, and elsewhere.

And it is just by reason of the enormous expenditure on vast prisons that the grievous and mischievous contrast arises between the comforts provided for murderers and men guilty of arson in their cells and the privations to which the honest poor are exposed in hospitals, poorhouses, town garrets, country hovels, and barracks. One of the most significant results which I noticed at the exhibition of various plans of cells in connection with the Prison Congress at Rome in 1885 was that it demonstrated to the general public how the cellular system treats prisoners (whether before trial or after sentence) better than the poor, who continue to be honest in spite of their wretchedness.[24]

[24] Even prison experts have been concerned by the vast expense of the cellular system, and the following question was brought forward at the Congress at Rome:-- ``What modifications would be possible, in accordance with recent experience, in the construction of cellular prisons so as to render it more simple and less costly, without detriment to the necessary conditions of a sound and intelligent application of the system?" Detailed recommendations were agreed to on the motion of M. Herbette;

but the system is unchanged, with requirements which can be only very slightly reduced.

In Germany, as well as in France and Italy, legislation has ordained, by codes and special laws, the cellular system for all punishment by imprisonment; but fortunately the system has not yet been adopted, thanks to its enormous cost. So that we have the further absurdity of codes based on prison systems which have no actual existence. And since criminals have their part in the law, not as it is written but as it is carried out, the result is naturally disastrous.

Thus the cellular system bears hard upon the honest classes, both by its enormous cost, under the form of taxation, and by competition with free and honest labour. The competition is moral in the first place, for the criminal is always assured of daily work, lodgings, and food, whilst the honest workman is assured of neither. Even the economic competition, though not extensive when we take the totals of free workmen and prisoners, is still very keen in particular places and for particular industries, whilst prison labour never indemnifies the State for its expenditure; for clearly with cellular isolation it is impossible to organise important and profitable industry. It is the small industries, such as shoemaking and carpentry, which crush the same free industries all round the prison, for they cannot stand against the artificial competition created by the nominal wages of the prison hands. Though for moral and financial reasons the convicts must work, it is evident that on these grounds we cannot accept the cellular system as a pattern of prison organisation.

It is quite sufficient, in prisons for the segregation of criminals, to provide for isolation by night, which requires buildings far more simple and less costly than those of the cellular prisons.

Work in the open air is the only useful basis of organisation for convict prisons.

Air, light, movement, field labour, especially in southern counties and for the majority of prisoners, who are rural--these are the only physical and moral disinfectants possible for prisoners not entirely degenerate, or likely to prevent at least the absolute brutalisation of the incorrigible, by giving them healthy and more remunerative work.

The penal agricultural colony, in lands which need clearing, is the best for adults, passing from the least to the most healthy according to the categories of criminals-- born, habitual, occasional--and according to the gravity of the crimes committed. To this may be added, for convicts less capable of restoration to social life, labour in mines, especially when the mines are State property. What I have said of malaria I say of fire-damp: it is much better that these should kill off criminals, than honest workmen.

The penal agricultural colony in lands already cultivated is best for children and young people.

This is the ideal and the typical form of segregation for criminals, against whom it would not be sufficient to exact strict reparation of damage, on the principles already set forth.

Wherever there is a crowding of humanity, there is human fermentation and putrefaction. Only labour in the open air will secure physical and moral health. And if agricultural work would be less fitted for criminals from the towns, there is no reason why an agricultural colony should not make itself as far as possible self-sufficing by means of workshops where prisoners could ply the trade to which they were accustomed when at liberty. For town convicts without a trade, such as vagabonds, beggars, and the like, on the ground of their muscular incapacity for hard and regular work, an agricultural colony is still the most fit, for it provides light and varied occupations, as the agricultural colonies of Holland, Belgium, and Austria bear witness.

The same evolution will take place in regard to the segregation of criminals as in regard to the seclusion of the insane; first, hospitals and prisons, with a terrible communion of corruption in both cases; then barrack life, in asylums or penitentiaries, vast and isolated; lastly, for the insane, a system of so-called village asylums, and even a free colony for harmless idiots who can be put to agricultural work and minor trades, as at Gheel in Belgium. Similarly for criminals, the sanitary ``elbow room" of agricultural colonies will be substituted for the infectious barrack-life of the great prisons.

As for habitual criminals, their anthropological characteristics remind us that we must distinguish between the two crises of their criminal activity, and, as a consequence, between the methods of defence against them. That is to say, we must distinguish between the initial moment at which they commit their first crime and the subsequent period in which they become habitual offenders, recidivists, and even incorrigible.

Thus it is clear that at the initial moment of their criminal career they ought to be subjected to the measures which I am about to indicate for occasional criminals; whereas, when from occasional they have become, partly by their imprisonment, habitual offenders, they must be subjected to the measures already indicated for born criminals. The latter are incorrigible through congenital tendency to degenerate, and the former are incorrigible through acquired tendency; but they end in the same degree of anti-sociality and brutalisation. There is, however, this difference, that habitual offenders nearly always commit less serious crimes, such as theft, swindling, forgery, indecent assault, whilst the born criminals, though they may be petty thieves, or not very formidable swindlers, are more frequently murderers, footpads, guilty of arson, or the like. Thus the discipline of their segregation must vary accordingly.

For occasional criminals, social defence must have a character of prevention rather than of repression, so as to save them from being driven, by a mistaken prison organisation, to become recidivists, and therefore habitual and incorrigible criminals.

It is especially important in this category to discriminate between the young and the adults, for with the former, far more than with the latter, the preventive methods may have a sensible effect in diminishing crime. But we must take care, in place of the pedantic graduation of responsibility which satisfies the penal codes, to substitute a physiological and psychical treatment of children and young people, who are actual criminals or framing for crime.

Beginning with the physical and moral treatment of foundling children as one of the most effectual penal substitutes, and advancing to reformatory constraint and penal sentences upon the young, there is an entire system crying for radical reform, from which imprisonment for young persons should always be excluded. We must therefore abolish the so-called houses of correction; for, taking no account of the absurd and dangerous confusion created by the three classes of children committed for paternal correction, for begging and vagrancy, and for offences, no good can ever come of it, for the herding and crowding together are nowhere more productive of fermentation and putrefaction than amongst the young.

There is nothing for them but separate boarding-out with families of honest country folk, or else agricultural colonies with a discipline different from that of the colonies for adult criminals, but still based on the rule of isolation by night, work in the open air, and as little crowding as possible.

For adult occasional criminals it is unnecessary to insist any further on the absurdity and danger of short terms of imprisonment, with or without isolation in cells, which now constitute the almost exclusive mode of repression. A few days in prison, mostly in association with habitual criminals, cannot exercise any deterrent influence, especially in the grotesque minimum of one day, or three days, as provided by the Dutch, Italian, and other codes. On the contrary, they are attended by disastrous effects, by destroying the serious character of justice, relieving prisoners of all fear of punishment, and consequently driving them to relapse, under the influence of the disgrace already suffered, and of the corrupting and compromising association with habitual criminals in prison.

The results of these short terms, indeed, which impose about the same restriction of liberty as an attack of indigestion, or a heavy fall of snow, are so manifest that the objection to them is now almost unanimous, though they still form the basis of the most recent penal codes.

As to the substitution of other repressive methods in the many cases of sentence for light offences, theorists and legislators have proposed domiciliary arrest, sureties, judicial warnings, compulsory work without imprisonment, conditional suspension of a sentence or a punishment, qualified banishment. For the moment there is a marked preference for conditional sentences.

In my opinion, however, none of these substitutes or short terms of imprisonment can be applied as effectively or as generally as is necessary for the large class of occasional offenders.

Domiciliary arrests, indeed, which the Italian penal code applies only to women and minors for a first contravention of the law, with detention in the house, cannot be made effective. They would be useless for those already obliged to remain at home by their daily occupations, and for the rich, who could have any form of distraction in their own houses; and they would be injurious to those who have to earn a living for themselves and their families in workrooms, shops, offices, &c. Moreover, this domiciliary detention would be very difficult in the great towns, where it would probably require a sentinel for every condemned person.

Bail for good behaviour is too unequal in the case of the poor and the rich, and therefore too rarely applicable to be any more than an exceptional and accessory measure, taken in conjunction with the payment of damages; and this even when it is given by sureties.

Judicial warning, with or without security, which the new Italian penal code has sought to revive, in spite of many years' experience under the older codes, cannot be seriously treated. Either the prisoner is an occasional offender, or an offender through passion, having a sense of honour, in which case public opinion is itself a sufficient lesson for him, without the need of a little moral lecture from the judge; or else he has no such moral sensibility, and then the warning is a mere useless ceremony, without effect either on the criminal or on the public. So true is this that judicial warning (a different thing from police warning, which is another so-called preventive measure, both ineffectual and injurious) is rarely applied by magistrates.

Compulsory work without imprisonment may be admitted, not as a main punishment, but as a mode of enforcing strict reparation of damage, which I still believe to be the only suitable measure for occasional offenders, when the offence is slight.

The same must be said for qualified banishment (temporary removal from the place where the crime was committed), which may be added as a preventive measure, and as a satisfaction for the injured party, in the same cases where the payment of damages is the principal retribution.

There remains the conditional sentence. A judge may decide, in the case of first offenders who appear to him to call for such treatment, that the sentence or the execution of the sentence, shall be suspended for a given period, after which, if the offender has been of good behaviour, and has not committed another offence, the sentence is effaced and the condemnation is regarded as non-existent; whilst in the other case the sentence takes effect, and the punishment is added to that of the new crime.

This conditional suspension, however, assumes two very different forms.

At Boston, in the State of Massachusetts, from the year 1870 in the case of minors, and from 1878 in the case of adults, judgment is suspended without regard even to the gravity of the crime or to the antecedents of the criminal; and this custom has applied to the entire State from the year 1880. All that the judge does is to fix the period of probation. There is a probation officer whose business it is to keep his eye on the persons affected, and who has extensive powers, including that of bringing them up for sentence even for disorderly conduct, without waiting for an actual relapse. This system has also been introduced into New Zealand and Australia (1886).

In England, after the advocacy of the probation system by the Howard Association, an Act was passed in 1887 ``to permit the conditional Release of first Offenders in certain cases." This law combines probation with sureties for good conduct. Judgment is given, but sentence is not pronounced. The suspension is not granted to any one who has previously committed an offence, or whose first offence would be liable to a punishment exceeding two years' imprisonment. There is no probation officer, for supervision is replaced by personal or other sureties for good behaviour.

On the continent of Europe another form has been adopted. There is no supervision by a special officer, and no surety for good behaviour; judgment is delivered and sentence pronounced; and the suspension is not forfeited by disorderly conduct, but only by an actual relapse.

This system, so far as the purpose was not effected by various conditions as to the duration of punishment, which left room for conditional sentences, as to the interval for taking cognisance of relapse, and other details, was proposed in France (1884) by Senator Berenger; but Belgium was the first country to adopt it in the law of 1888 ``on conditional release and conditional sentences;" and France followed in 1891, with the law ``on the modification and increase of punishments."

Before that time, at the Prison Congresses of London (1872) and Rome (1885), there had been some discussion, without resolutions, on the advisability of substituting for punishment with hard labour either simple detention without labour or compulsory labour without imprisonment, or removal from the place where the offence was committed, or judicial admonition.

But the most noteworthy advocacy of conditional sentences, after the action taken by the Howard Association in 1881, came from the International Union of Penal Legislation, which at its Conference at Berne in 1889 adopted a resolution in its favour, whilst insisting, at the suggestion of M. Garofalo, ``on the necessity of deciding its limitation according to local conditions, and to the public opinion and moral characteristics of various nations."

The Prison Congress of St. Petersburg discussed the substitution of judicial admonition or conditional sentences for short terms of imprisonment; but no resolution could be arrived at on this occasion, and the matter was postponed to the next international Prison Congress (Paris, 1895).

In Austria and Germany, again, several Bills have been introduced, dealing with conditional sentences.

There are statistics for Belgium on the operation of this system. The law of 1888 requires the keeper of the seals to report annually to Parliament; and that authority drew up two reports, dated May 14, 1890, and July 7, 1891.

From the day when the law came into operation up to December 31, 1889, out of 61,787 sentences in the Correctional Tribunals, 8,696 were conditional; and there were 192 relapses. Out of 222,492 sentences in the Police Courts, 4,499 were conditional, and there were 45 relapses.

These 13,195 conditional sentences included 8,485 for crimes and offences under the penal code; 2,286 for breaches of police regulations; 447 for breaches of communal and provincial regulations; and 1,977 for contraventions of special laws.

The crimes and offences for which these sentences have been most frequently pronounced are as follows:--

Correctional. Police.

Malicious Wounding ... ... 3,339 ... 491 Thefts, &c ... ... 1,803 ... 206 Resistance to and attacks on Authorities 961 ... 67 Destruction of Inclosures and Property 211 ... 56 Swindling and Breach of Trust ... ... 125 ... 5 Slander and Defamation ... ... 113 ... 79 Immorality ... ... 112 ... 10

Offences below 100 were: Abusive language, 99; Indecent assaults, 59; Threats, 58; Forgery, 49; Adultery, 48; Adulteration of food, 44; Unlawful wounding, 45;

Unlawful possession, 31; Unlawful carrying and sale of arms, 30; Bankruptcy, 26; Accidental homicide, 20.

In the year 1890, out of 41,330 sentences in the Correctional Tribunals, whereof 36,660 were not over six months' imprisonment, 7,932 were conditional, and there were 223 relapses. Out of 121,461 in the Police Courts, 6,377 were conditional, and there were 49 relapses.

The proportion for various offences was approximately the same as in the previous year.

These figures, it is true, do not tell us much about the effects of conditional sentences in Belgium, as we might expect from the brevity of the experiment; so that the question still remains in the theoretical phase.

The statistics of the Massachusetts probation system are not much more instructive.

According to the decennial report (1879-88) of Mr. Savage, probation officer at Boston, imprisonment was remitted in the county of Suffolk (including Boston) to 322 persons in 1879 and to 880 in 1888; whilst the number officially recorded for the following year was 994. In the course of ten years the probation officer inquired into the cases of 27,052 persons liable to supervision. Of these, 7,251 were put on probation, and 580 were deprived of the benefit of the law.

The grounds on which the probation system was applied in Massachusetts were strikingly different from the circumstances under which conditional sentences were recorded in Belgium. Thus in Boston there were put on probation, between 1879 and 1888, 3,161 persons charged with drunkenness for the first time, 222 charged with habitual drunkenness, 211 with drunkenness for the third time, 958 with theft, 764 with solicitation, 470 with inflicting bodily harm, 274 with disorderly conduct and idleness, 240 with violation of domicile, especially with intrusion in business premises.

Thus, apart from the difference of penal legislation and social life in the two countries, the Boston system is applied mainly to drunkards, who are not true criminals by the mere fact of intoxication.

As for the statistics of ascertained relapse, which in Boston reached 64 out of 1,125 (6 per cent.) in 1889, I think they should be received with caution. In the case of every new penal or penitentiary system or measure, we never fail to receive more or less wonderful figures on the results obtained; but the common fate of all these splendid results has always been that they dwindle down, even if they do not turn into a negative quantity, so as to indicate the necessity of other more practical and serviceable measures. The reason is, and will continue to be the same, namely, that legislators, judges, and prison warders have no adequate knowledge of criminals, and their activity is anything but harmonious. This accounts for the superficial character, if nothing more, of the measures which are taken, and which apply far more to the crime than to the criminal, without so much as touching the true and deep-seated roots of crime. Hence also the inevitable disillusion, almost before the new device is a month old.

I by no means admit the two principal objections of MM. Kirchenheim and Wach, that the conditional sentence is repugnant to the principle of absolute justice, according to which every offence should be visited by a corresponding punishment, and that short terms of imprisonment, if they have not always produced a good result, ought not to be abolished, but only applied in a more suitable and efficacious manner.

The first objection will not weigh much with those who are guided by the principles and method of the positive school. As M. Gautier says, it is absolutely useless to dispute about consequences when we start from premises so opposed to each other as retributive justice, according to which every fault demands a proportional punishment--``fiat justitia pereat mundus"--and social defence, according to which a justice without social advantage is an unjust justice, afflicted with metaphysical degeneracy.

The second objection appears to me to have no better foundation, for the disadvantages of punishments by short terms of imprisonment are organic and inevitable defects. There is no chance of their practical amelioration, for they have all been tried, from the system of association to that of absolute isolation, from the most inflexible vigour to the mildest treatment. Amelioration of short-term punishments can only have an indirect influence by way of palliation; but it is the actual imprisonment for a short term which is trifling and unavailing.

At the same time, and not to mention other objections on points of detail, specially applicable to the form given to conditional sentences on the continent of Europe, as compared with the American system, (which is certainly better, since it does not leave the offender to himself, and is not restricted to the simple legal relapse), I am not enthusiastically in favour of the conditional sentence. And my lack of enthusiasm, in spite of the first impression, which was decidedly favourable, is based on different grounds from those hitherto stated by the opponents of this reform.

In the earliest edition of this work I maintained that repression ought to be mild in form for occasional criminals, and progressively severe for recidivists and habitual evildoers, until it reached perpetual segregation. The Italian proverb, that ``the first fault is pardoned and the second whipped," is an unconscious confirmation of the popular opinion. And from this point of view the conditional sentence, if combined as in the French law with progressive severity of repression for recidivists, is sufficiently attractive in the first instance.

But the conditional sentence, to consider it for a moment as it has hitherto been propounded and carried out, has two characteristic defects, in common with the actual penal system, of which its advocates, for the most part balancing between the classical and positive school, cannot get rid.

In the first place, whilst the classical school has fixed its attention on crime, and the positive school studies the criminal, especially in regard to his biological and psychological character, the advocates of the conditional sentence (and of the laws which have so far brought it into operation) oscillate between the two standpoints, considering the criminal, no doubt, rather than the crime, but only the average and abstract criminal, not the living and palpitating criminal, as he is to be found in his several categories. In proof of this it is enough to observe that the ninth article of the Belgian law admits the conditional sentence, so far as punishment is concerned, when this punishment does not exceed six months, EVEN IF THE PERIOD IS MADE UP BY THE CUMULATION OF TWO OR MORE! In other words, the conditional sentence is allowed in the case of a criminal who has committed several offences--which substantially (except in the few cases of connected offences due to the same action, or arising out of the same occasion) is a mere case of relapse, and therefore proves in the majority of cases that the law is not dealing with true occasional criminals; for these, as a rule, like criminals of passion, only commit a single crime or offence.

The two fundamental conditions of the conditional sentence in Europe (a slight infraction and a nonrelapsed criminal) do not, therefore, afford a complete guarantee of the utility of its application.

It is true that this system tends to fix the attention of the judge on the personal conditions of the prisoner, requiring him to decide if the conditional sentence is suitable to the particular occasion, having regard to the special circumstances of the action and the individual, apart from the legal limitations of the offence and of the punishment.

But we know that the crowding of the prisons with persons condemned to short terms of imprisonment is attended by a grievous crowding in the courts of prisoners accused of slight offences and contraventions. Thus it is inevitable that the judges, even apart from their ignorance of the biological and psychological characters of the offenders, being compelled to decide ten or twenty cases every day, cannot fix their attention on the procession of figures which files past the magic lantern of the courts, but simply leave them with a ticket bearing the number of the article which applies, not to THEM, but to their particular infraction of the law. Thus the judges will come to pronouncing the conditional sentence almost mechanically, just as they have come to give the benefit of attenuating circumstances by force of habit This device also was introduced in France in 1832, in order to ``individualise punishment''--that is to say, to compel the judge to apply his sentence rather to the criminal than to the crime.

So long as penal procedure is not radically reformed, as we have proposed, in such a manner that the inquiry, the discussion, the decision upon the evidence, which are the only proper elements of penal justice, aim at and lead up to the determination of a prisoner's biological and psychological type, it will be humanly impossible for the practical application of these judicial measures to overcome the mechanical impersonality of justice, which applies rather to the crime than to the criminal.

Hence the conditional sentence, though it was evolved by the abuse and disastrous effects of short terms of imprisonment, and in spite of its generating principle that ``the first fault is pardoned and the second whipped,'' has to-day only the character of an eclectic graft on the old classic stock of penal law and procedure. As such, notwithstanding its attractive features (for it indicates a step in advance towards the positive system of social defence, which desires to see the application of collective defence to the individual's power of offence), it seems to me to be destined, not long after its earliest application, to deceive the anticipations of happy and beneficent results, such as its advocates entertain.

Moreover, the conditional sentence, precisely because it is a graft on the old classic stock of penal justice, has another very serious defect, inasmuch as it overlooks the victims of the offence.

Its advocates, in fact, continue to maintain that reparation of damage is a private concern, for which they benevolently recommend a strict remedy, but which they nevertheless, in practice, entirely overlook.

The offender who is conditionally sentenced is, therefore, to secure a suspension of punishment--which, indeed, it is as well to remember, he also secures, often enough, by a legal limitation, or, as in Italy, by the remission of punishments under three months, accorded whenever (as is generally the case) there is a petition for pardon. But is there any one who gives a thought to the victims?

From this point of view it may even be said that the conditional sentence makes things worse than before; for the victims are not to have so much as the satisfaction of seeing punishment inflicted on those who have injured them, in cases of assault, theft, swindling, and the like. And it is useless to make the platonic remark, as M. Fayer has done, that punishment is punishment even when conditional, and involves the censure of the public authority, and holds in reserve a punishment for relapse, and hangs over the head of the offender until his term of probation has expired.

159

All this is pretty enough--except the relapse, which implies the poor consolation of a repetition of the offence, which would be no great satisfaction for the victims of the first. But it is all hypothetical and theoretical. The essential thing, so far as the victims are concerned, is that the offender goes unpunished.

It is true that occasional offenders deserve consideration, from the point of view of prevention in particular; but honest folk who are injured by them deserve it still more.

I do not therefore agree with Garofalo, who proposed at Brussels that the conditional sentence should be subject to the consent of the injured party; but I think that it ought not to be permitted until there has been an indemnification for the victims of the offence, or at least a guarantee, either by the offender, or directly by the State.

In short, for occasional criminals who commit slight offences, in circumstances which show that they are not of a dangerous type, I say, as I have said already, that reparation of the damage inflicted would suffice as a defensive measure, without a conditional sentence of imprisonment

As to the occasional criminals who commit serious offences, for which reparation alone would not be sufficient, temporary removal from the scene of the crime should be added in the less serious cases, whilst in the cases of greater gravity, owing to material and personal considerations, there should be indefinite segregation in an agricultural colony, with lighter work and milder discipline than those prescribed in colonies for born criminals and recidivists.

The last category is that of criminals through an impulse of passion, not anti-social but susceptible of excuse, such as love, honour, and the like.

For these individuals all punishment is clearly useless, at any rate as a psychological counteraction of crime, for the very conditions of the psychological convulsion which caused them to offend precludes any deterrent influence in a legal menace.

I therefore believe that in typical cases of criminals of passion, where there is no clear demand for mental treatment in a criminal lunatic asylum, imprisonment is of no use whatever. Strict reparation of damage will suffice to punish them, whilst they are punished already by genuine and sincere remorse immediately after the criminal explosion of their legitimate passion. Temporary removal from the scene of their crime and from the residence of the victim's family might be superadded.

Nevertheless it must not be forgotten that I say this in connection with criminals in whom the passionate impulse is really exceptional, and who present the physiological and psychical features of the genuine criminal of passion which I enumerated in the first chapter.

I come to a different conclusion in the case of criminals who have merely been provoked, who do not completely present these features, who are actuated by a combination of social and excusable passion with an anti-social passion, such as hate, vengeance, anger, ambition, &c. Of such a kind are murderers carried away by anger just in itself, by blood-feuds, or desire to avenge the honour of their family, by vindication of personal honour, by grave suspicion of adultery, &c.; persons guilty of malicious wounding, disfigurement through erotic motives, and the like. These may be classed as occasional criminals, and treated accordingly.

Such, then, in general outline, is the positive system of social, preventive, and repressive defence against crimes and criminals, in accordance with the inferences from a scientific study of crime as a natural and social phenomenon.

It is a defensive system which, in the nature of things, must of necessity be substituted for the criminal and penitentiary systems of the classical school, so soon as the daily experience of every nation shall have established the conviction, which at this moment is more or less profound, but merely of a general character, that these systems are henceforth incompatible with the needs of society, not only by their crude pedantry, but also because their consequences are becoming daily more disastrous.